THE WORD IS HERE

Keorapetse Kgositsile was born in 1938 in Johannesburg, South Africa. He is a poet and essayist and has been living in exile since 1961. Mr. Kgositsile was on the staff of *New Age*, a now-banned South African political weekly. He is the recipient of the second Conrad Kent Rivers Memorial Poetry Award, given by *Black World* magazine. He has published three volumes of poetry entitled, *Spirits Unchained*, *For Melba*, and *My Name Is Afrika*.

THE WORD IS HERE
Poetry from Modern Africa

EDITED BY
KEORAPETSE KGOSITSILE

ANCHOR BOOKS

Doubleday & Company, Inc., Garden City, New York, 1973

Anchor Books Edition: 1973

ISBN: 0-385-01516-x
Library of Congress Catalog Card Number 70–186034
Copyright © 1973 by Doubleday & Company, Inc.
All Rights Reserved
Printed in the United States of America

First Edition

All efforts have been made to secure the proper permission for each selection
in this anthology. However, if some of the selections are not properly ac-
knowledged, please contact Doubleday & Company, Inc., in order to clarify
the situation.

Grateful acknowledgment is made to the following for permission to reprint
poems contained in this anthology:

Ama Ata Aidoo for her "Cornfields in Accra," reprinted by permission of Ama
Ata Aidoo and *The New African*.

Kofi Awoonor for "Desire," "The Cathedral," "Delight of Tears," and
"Lament of the Silent Sister" from *Night of My Blood* by Kofi Awoonor.
Copyright © 1971 by Kofi Awoonor. Reprinted by permission of Double-
day & Company, Inc.

Dennis Brutus for "Letters to Martha #1, #2, #6, #7, #9, #11,
#14," and "Presumably." Reprinted by permission of Heinemann Edu-
cational Books, Ltd., London, England.

J. P. Clark for "Song," "Seasons of Omens," "Skulls and Cups," "Dirge,"
"Death of a Weaverbird," "Party Song," "The Casualties," and "To
My Academic Friends Who Sit Tight on Their Doctoral Theses and
Have No Chair for Poet or Inventor," from *Casualties: Poems 1966–
1968* by J. P. Clark. Copyright © 1970 by J. P. Clark. Reprinted by
permission of the Africana Publishing Corporation, New York.

Solomon Deressa for "Prayer," "Intersection," "Poem," "Ring the Child
Alive," "Why?," "Similitudes," "The Dry Well," "Poem," and "Poem,"
from *Prayer, Ring the Child Alive* (1969). Reprinted by permission
of the author.

David Diop for "For My Mother," "The Vultures," "Times," "With You,"
"The Renegade," "Africa," "Rama Kam," and "Negro Tramp." Re-
printed from *Journal of the New African Literature and the Arts*, The

Third Press, Joseph Okpaku Publishing Co., Inc., New York. Copyright © 1970, 1968 by the *Journal of African Literature and the Arts*, J. Okpaku, publisher.

Zweli ed Dladla for "Sacrilege to Self," "Dribbling Around," "A Song of Hope," "Inertia," "Epitaph on Faces," "It Happened," "The Wilderness," and "Land of the Lull." Reprinted by permission of the author.

Keorapetse Kgositsile for "Origins," "Tropics," and "For Melba." Reprinted by permission of Third World Press, Chicago, Illinois. Also, "To Mother," "For Eusi, Ayi Kwei & Gwen Brooks," and "The New Breed." From *My Name Is Afrika* by Keorapetse Kgositsile. Reprinted by permission of Doubleday & Company, Inc.

Mazisi Kunene for "Anthem of Decades (extract from an Epic), Part I" and "The Gold-miners," from *Zulu Poems* by Mazisi Kunene. Copyright © 1970 by Mazisi Kunene. Reprinted by permission of the Africana Publishing Corporation, New York.

Burns Machobane for "Ode to Little Johnny's Dream," "False Brothers," and "Lament." Reprinted by permission of the author.

Edouard Maunick for "As Far as Yoruba Land" which was published in No. 55 (3rd Quarterly 1965) of the revue *Presence Africaine*, Paris, France.

Ifeanyi Menkiti for "Veterans Day," which appeared in *Okike* magazine, "Adaiba," which appeared in *Nigeria* magazine and "Age of the Gods Who Never Came," which appeared in *African Arts* magazine. Reprinted by permission of the author. Also for "For Malcolm," "Blonde Bondage," "Grace Before Meal," "The Drunken Priest," "And All Shall Be Well," and "The Pagans Sat Still," reprinted by permission of Third World Press, 1972.

Stella Ngatho for "Foot-path," "The Kraal," and "A Young Tree." Reprinted by permission of the author.

Christopher Okigbo for "Thunder Can Break," "Elegy of the Wind," "Come Thunder," "Hurray for Thunder," "Elegy for Slit-Drum," and "Elegy for Alto." Copyright © 1968 by Christopher Okigbo, from *Labyrinths* by Christopher Okigbo. Reprinted by permission of the Legal Personal Representatives of Christopher Okigbo, the Africana Publishing Corporation and Heinemann Educational Books, Ltd., London, England.

Okot p'Bitek for "My Husband's House Is a Dark Forest of Books" from *Song of Lawino* by Okot p'Bitek. Reprinted by permission of the East African Publishing House, Nairobi, Kenya.

David Rubadiri for "The Tide That from the West Washes Africa to the Bone," "On Meeting a West Indian Boat Train at Waterloo Station," "Thoughts After Work," "Ogunoba's Talking Drum," and "Kampala Beggar," from *Pergamon Poets II—Poetry From Africa* (1968). Reprinted by permission of the author.

Wole Soyinka for "Koko Oloro," "Post Mortem," "Black Singer," and "Civilian and Soldier" from *Idandre and Other Poems* by Wole Soyinka. Reprinted by permission of Hill and Wang, a division of Farrar, Straus, and Giroux.

Tchikaya U Tam'si for "Brush-fire," "Three Poems from *Epitomé*," and "The Scorner" from *Modern Poetry From Africa* edited by Moore and Beier. Reprinted by permission of the author.

This book is dedicated to the memory of Magolwane, Langston Hughes, Zora Neale Hurston, Chris Okigbo & Can Themba—dream keepers & weaverbirds all

CONTENTS

FROM THE CENTER

Introduction

The word, as a cultural implement, is a vehicle that carries us to some kernel of meaning to shape our thought and feeling in order for us to be better able to act to shape our life with some clarity of understanding past mere deadweight knowledge. The word then, in the service of the poet's vision, proposes certain relationships in whatever area of experience the poet has isolated to explore or celebrate in song. Thus the poem, finally, affirms, proposes or opposes certain values.

Poetry, the word at its most expressive, can be a prayer, an appeal, condemnation, encouragement, affirmation—the list of endeavors is endless. And if it is authentic, as anything else expressive of a people's spirit, it is always social.

That *social* should tell us something about the orientation of the poetry, what it proposes to do and, therefore, the poet's intended audience. The publishers of African poetry are overwhelmingly Euro-American. The greater bulk of the poetry in this anthology, as in all the anthologies contributed to by contemporary African writers, is of European expression, that is, English, French, Portuguese. So one is tempted to ask: Who is the audience of the contemporary African writer? The bored Euro-American liberal literati searching for literary exotica in the African quarters of their empire? The African elite trained away from themselves in institutions of European design? Who? You see, the audience whose approval an artist seeks is influential on the artist's vision—the totality of his thinking, feeling and understanding of his responsibilities, his commitment, his allegiances, his values, both ethical and aesthetic.

And poetry, as any other art form, as social comment, serves an educational purpose. In our time then, the African poet is either a tool of oppression or seeks to be an agent of liberation.

Since the advent of slavery and colonization, African poetry, as everything else African that was not for European profit or fun, has suffered. As Kunene has pointed out: "The conquest of the African people led to frantic attempts by both missionaries and administrators to eliminate traditional values, except where they furthered the interests of the conquerors. Inevitably this led to the destruction of the very institutions which acted as a creative force. . . . the administrator continuously preached the superiority of his way of life. Through western books, with their highly biased accounts of history, he blocked any possibilities of self-discovery. A people grew up whose whole ethos was of foreign derivation, who not only aspired to the things of 'the white man' but also looked at its own history with revulsion. . . . What happened in the missionary schools was even more tragic in so far as African traditional literature and culture was concerned. The missionary and the administrator combined efforts to promulgate rules by which African language and traditional cultural expressions (such as dancing, 'excited participation' and 'body exposure') were forbidden at the risk of incurring serious punishment such as hard labour and ridicule. On the other hand, English language, English country dances, and English styles of clothing were yoked round the necks of the pupils."

What Kunene is saying about Zulu literature and culture is true of all African institutions—politics, philosophy, religion, education, economics, sex, almost whatever you can

think of, since the missionary and the colonial administra-
tor set their ominous feet on African soil. What this means,
finally, is that what happens in Africa today is not always
necessarily African, even when the people who are involved
are African. This applies as much to poetry as it does to
any other activity and the uses of our energies.

So this anthology is a small reflection of poetry in Africa
today.

THE WORD IS HERE. I have tried to gather it from all
over Africa, not to reflect my preferences but to reflect the
pulse of Africa today.

What you do with words is a very precise indicator of
where you are, where you want to be. Although many
African writers have been damaged by the violence with
which European values were imposed on us, and they have
ended up imitating Western literary styles and forms, some
have survived this assault. Kunene, for instance, makes his
poetry in Zulu, and he is very conscious of the tradition
out of which he works, the tradition in whose fertile soil
his poetry is deeply rooted. He then translates into "Eng-
lish" in order to publish his work for an English-dominated
readership, thus being forced to murder a great deal of the
intense internal rhythms of his Zulu poems. p'Bitek wrote
Song of Lawino in Acoli, and did what Kunene does, thus
rendering "the sharp edges of the warrior's sword rusty and
blunt." U Tam'si writes in "French" but bends it to be as
close to African expression as he can make it, in very much
the same way that the authentic Black musician in America
has used European musical instruments to express the
depth of Black feeling he is connected to. There are more.
All this is us today. All this is very logical.

FROM THE NORTH

Here we begin again
We are everywhere more
Shattered than any independence
Guidebook would have guts to say

Le Foehn

Mouloud Mammeri

Here is the sea
With her full sails,
There where the sun does not the sky abandon
Even for a few months
Without regret.
Rows of white terrace houses nourished by heat
Up on that abrupt hill, it is the Casbah.
Further, the new town
Heaves against the sky
Basalt pillars of her skyscrapers.
Stranger, you are here
Facing the Whitest of towns . . .
White Algiers . . .
But
Poetry should not seduce you in itself:
In the gleaming whiteness of that town
In truth,
Men pursue prosaic lives
And only die with drama.
Look at that door:
It is closed.
It is there that the hours, the knocks, the misfortunes
Will enter.
Behind the screen of that closed door
The actors wait for the hour to strike
And their destiny is set.
Because
When too much dryness burns their hearts
When hunger wrings their entrails
When one suppresses too many tears
When one stifles too many dreams

It is as though one piles log upon log on a funeral pyre:
In the end, it needs only one slave
In all God's heaven
And in the hearts of men, to cause
The most enormous incendiary.
Listen:
Against that closed door
They do not wait for destiny's approval:
It is yet peaceful . . .
Useless for you to decry men's silence:
Each morning they have the rendezvous with the sun,
Coffee with milk, a pat of butter, the fresh croissants
Or a crust of bread and figs.
Does it matter what!
These are the coffee, the butter, bread, and the figs of silence
The men make love, some father babies
They calculate the end of months
Wait for Saturday to go to the stadium
To play at war
The war where there are only heroes and no casualties.
In the bars of that town called the White City
The town of white islands
They return each night to the rendezvous they've kept for years
They sip white aniseed
They pick up the same kemias
From the counters of the same bistros.
The boys guy the girls
The girls entice the boys
And they laugh
As one laughs in peace
Because tomorrow they know the same procession of passive
    gestures
Will resume
And they are the new rendezvous with the sun
The blue sky
The mauve sea

The streets
Of the whitest of all white cities . . .
And still . . .
Still it needs only
A few steps by an aimless walker
To change the world.
Because to those few strides some other men
Born under the same blue skies
And after an even longer time,
So long they cannot remember,
Some other men
Panting from the gloom of the morning
Roll toward the crest of the hill
The hump which they know
Will deliver them to the plain.
They divide the days
They no longer wait for dawn.
They've found in the quarter all streets impassable;
They follow others
To give some semblance of going somewhere.
You know what that is:
A man is someone who has somewhere to go.
When a man has the impression he has nowhere to go
He dies,
Or he kills.
It is so long since the men of this strange city knew
They were going nowhere.
They make the rounds, their eyes fixed to the ground,
Because they fear to look at the sun,
To be dazzled.
They stumble in the maze of the same impasses
And they retrace their steps
They criss-cross their fruitless paths
On the same false crossroads
From whence begin again
Their hopeless journeys.

Even words they give themselves are false:
Their city, from the time it was theirs,
They called it "The Well-Guarded"!
Oh, what derision! What a joke!
Their "well-guarded" island has become the boulevard of covetors
Rushing to hopeless horizons
And their city an estranged city in which
They blunder like strangers.
It is more than a century since
That city has thus absurdly lived,
One half lowering at the other half.
That can no longer continue.
The doped happiness of others
No longer calms the others' disquiet;
The happy ones of the white town
Find their joy turned to ashes
And wish the other would turn
Would cease to look
Or, better still, cease to exist.
But the others . . .
The others know much, much too late
The forbidden paradise begins at Bresson Square,
That one incursion into rue d'Isly is a raid into enemy territory
Who are vowed to cover up their misery in the swarming crowds
    of all the miserable ones of the Casbah.
They have intervals of lucidity
Or of despair
Or some mad elations,
A mad wish to kill
To die
And with all their heart, all their blood, they wish
The other would cease to look
Or merely cease to exist . . .
The evening promenade of the young wolves dies at the side
    of the Café Sourbiron,
At Tantonville, it stops and retraces itself:

It has struck against a wall.

The wanderings of the famished young jackals
Faulters on the invisible bulwark
Under the pressure of others
And the shoving of others
The curtain begins to crack . . .
It has cracked!
And on the asphalt of the same streets
The young jackals and the young wolves
No longer come to blows at night,
Nor is the day for bravado.
Also
That folding screen,
The frail folding screen of that door yields,
And . . .

TRANSLATED BY LEWIS NKOSI

As Far as Yoruba Land

Edouard Maunick

FOREWORD

Where this poem? . . .

In Nigeria, in the town of Oshogbo, towards midday, or a little later. I had driven at breakneck speed with Wole Soyinka. I learnt from him, the meaning of Ofatedo we had crossed, coming from Ibadan: "the place where the bow and arrow rest," he uttered between two steps on the gas. I noted on the corner of an envelope, as a neophyte. Was I already convinced that Ofatedo would serve to feed the poem? . . . Maybe!

Reaching Oshogbo, Ulli Beier did the honours of the place to me. He took me to the temple of Oshun that had known a real restoration, through a revival of the faith of the inhabitants of the country. They had learnt to mould cement. Using and abusing forms, colours, and, above all, their belief in bringing back to life the sacred arpent, they had once more succeeded to stare the unstarable: God.

Ulli Beier kept on talking: he was explaining to me every ikon, every pattern in the wall protecting the temple. He was letting me into the secrets of Oshun's worship: SHE had promised to the victorious warrior from Ibokun, to watch over the kingdom of Oshogbo, if the latter accepted not to build his palace on the place of the shrine, but a little farther, on the hillside. Moreover, she had convinced him of coming to feed the fish of the river nearby, once every year. He held out his hands to receive the first fish, and his name was born: Ataoja. I listened astonished. The silence of dead leaves, the vertical of trees, the barenness of their roots the water stark and stiff under the weight of branches sleeping between life and death, the statues and the patterns "strange as belief in God," the wall paradoxically enlarging the sacred space, and Ulli Beier, the Westerner having upset his identity: all this took me far away. Very far away, in my native island, Mauritius (*stella clavisque maris indici*), in Black River, kingdom of the African metizos, "the Mozambiques" as they are called, all of them fishermen, familiar to the fish, accomplices of the sea and sega dancers. Far back to my christening "my christian name uttered against time," "my head bowed over bowl of stone, unexpected jordan . . ." And farther back, to Gethsemane, "in the Other Garden." And my head started swimming: I yielded to the warning vertigo: the poem shooting his first bullets. Now that it is written, peace is back, having installed the reverse of "the brutal game of knowledge and of doubt": the consciousness that nothing Else is adultery but faith itself. I am from everywhere: from the West of reason and of Christ, from India contemplative and igneous, from Africa animistic and louder than voice of judge: I have written this poem.

As far as yoruba land, my birth has tracked me, challenging the word-beyond to the point of trial: I fell but did not fail.

Where this poem and when? . . .

Deep in myself, among the vulnerable midday of a man in search of a love he dreams to give to others in order to love himself a little: "I am not of the game, but THE game . . ."

As far as yoruba land, my contradiction: my wealth . . .

I

do not point the finger of scorn at yoruba land
call at the bar but the stranger
he has gone on the journey
from the depth of anxiety
his testimony combines only with memory
Oshogbo liberates the past
as a sower opens her hand
right hand
median town
goddess-line-of-life
the place is nowhere
without the place of Oshun.

II

and behold I have ransacked
the geography before the duration
the past is an acre
unbounded by the wall
water anoints the frontier
I dub you loaf as bread
a loaf of bread
saliva on your brow the legend
more limpid than honey of first hive
than river sleep-stricken
ancient ancient
more limpid more ancient than word of man.

III

I have named the place of Oshun
its kneeling river
—did you know that water breathed
because fed with branches
many deaths old—

I have named the place of Oshun
its wall contradicting all walls
—to enter I uttered sesames
simple as surprise—
I have named the place of Oshun
but not its trees cryptogamous
having lost their genesis perhaps.

IV

there came the warrior who came from Ibokun
do not speak of war
life was born after weapons
when the entrails are exhausted
knocking against the skin against night
do not speak of war
I have seized the bows
filled the quivers with images and proverbs
there the king held out his hands
there he received the fish
here began his name
here came Ataoja who came from Ibokun.

V

because they had lost their genesis
the trees were prohibited from me
—they are surely the high priests
who installed Oshun
before solitude
before the ritual—
the barks remained sealed books
—perhaps guardians forgotten granted
who stared at Oshun
before the ikon
before the dance—
was it to teach me the blood? . . .

VI

for there is an african virtue of the tree
that shares the stranger by way of baptism
—this time I felt it familiar
another noon but as if repeated
a poem recopied
a re-spouting—
how old is then the traveller
who is not as old as his name
but as old as all the gods encountered
all the temples
all the initiations
and among the crowd all the faces . . .

VII

I beckoned myself from the sacred acre
from baptism visible
from water touchable and touched
if you acted one day the same gesture!
a name reveals itself at the edge of the earth
living as green leaf
equally flesh
equally promised
I have a little preceded its season
thirty-three years in support
had we frequented the same storm? . . .

VIII

don't expect silence from me
or the tam-tam speech you are fond of
this name I'll tell ransacking my proverbs
a way of being negro without accent
I broke it to you skin-burning words
carrying the gangrene

the motive most ancient
but outlining the estuary
by dint of undertows
this place expected me for a new departure
I crossed Ofatedo
the town where the bow and arrow rest.

IX

Ofatedo
look up for it on the skin of Africa
Africa
find it glued on the belt of the World
the World
see it on the face of Man
Man
increase his excessiveness to poetry
his first reality his chance
Ofatedo as worthy as Elsinore
and all words stuffed with temptation
Ofatedo at least the stillness of arms.

X

I am from everywhere
I had to be from Oshogbo
and from all kingdoms dead or living
there the wall unbounds the frontier
it bears human traces
strange as belief in God
I have understood nothing I have lived everything
I speak of this share obscure
that keeps on surviving
this survival equal to oracles
I have visited Oshun
and behold my piety is adultery.

XI

of all kingdoms dead or living
opening on the sea
to the sea never forsaken
of all kingdoms
I unveil the names
daring is a wound
that must be opened as is scuttled
the penalty of dying
for one god or for another
I think of Oshun's breasts
two padlocked fruits
one must have seen them to be king.

XII

and this king in everyone of us
never banished
because free to choose his banishment
he hardly crosses my sleep
in this place where I do not sleep
but accomplice of appearances
I know its weight of secret beam
supporting noon—the star
then the bells of blood a-ringing
we start from Ibokun unconciously
spied upon by water the sacrament
our original suzerainty.

XIII

free from the brutal game
of knowledge and of doubt
back to my intimate story
explaining my birth
on the appointed day of equinox

of a september step by step
patiently agreed
a shadow breaks
with a snap as childhood
another game breaks out
the action of a chalice
on a party wall.

XIV

tell Gethsemane in yoruba land
I have transgressed the difficult
cast my memory back to the Other Garden
crossed the prohibited trees
without the crowd vociferating
and my eyes on Oshun
came without passion
to disaccomplish quest after quest
I was free to walk
neither back nor ahead
but in the action of a blade
with all my body reinvest the Bible.

XV

and it was like formerly in the Island
lightning foretold every year
the sweeping wind
that penetrates to the bone of the house
and the house restored
man having survived
I say like formerly in the Island
my head bowed over bowl of stone
unexpected jordan and salt of the sea
my christian name uttered against time
for a river celebrated every year
I rediscover the identity and the cathedral.

XVI

I have understood nothing I have lived everything
and it is difficult to me to relate
however I hunger so hunger for telling
will the word come at the end of the verse
will the psalm be sung with a good voice
and will the poem be able to cheat
in me and among you royally cheat
the answer is here
between Oshun and I
between me and my christening
half-bred half-bred to the very end
I dare murmur the hard hard word.

XVII

yesterday tempted to walk on fire
fortified by Siva and a pilgrimage
accomplished unknown to the flesh
somewhere towards Benares
running in the veins of the grandfather
to-day Oshun like a thorn
a clear call of sega
a temptation as old as Mozambique
blow dealt by the black great grandmother
right in the loins
and at all times the familiar
the welcome the crier of Tiberias.

XVIII

and I have chosen the no man's land of the sea
but behold every shore every land
is a fidelity to try
I say I am not of the game but the game
how is the weather amongst you
who do not know my alternations

my seasons my dance prayers
what weight of bread will you place on the table
what weight of rice and what weight of water
for I'll eat with you and I'll be thirsty
send for the sorcerer
and let him show our brotherly blood.

XIX

join in the round
I have got hands in store for every one of you
the mask has died waiting for me
do not point the finger of scorn at yoruba land
I shall be my only witness
I have gone on the journey from the depth of anxiety
in search of a lost genesis
Oshun stood on my way
I have beckoned myself from her sacred acre
my entrails are still throbbing
for having unduly withstood the dance prayer
join in the round and let us start the trial over again.

Fire That Is the Secret

Kateb Yacine

In the raised fist of youth
In the pert faces of unfledged heroines
In the struggle under the stars
In the fifth year of the massacre

The starred banner once again has found its origins
Algeria is freer than ever
She has always been free

In front of the waking people
The slaughterers parade
Their legions of mad dogs

Tears would flow
But the eyes remain open
It is not the Morice line
That kills
It is the well-fed mortar

Faces
what fire created you
So cruelly confident

This fire
That is the secret of all the sacrifices
Everywhere they pour out
And come forth
Of the peasants without land
And the old man comes out of his ruins
To offer his last sheep

Tonight we dance in the glow
Of tomorrow's battle

That fire
That is the secret of all the sacrifices

The day dawns
Forget misery
The rags
The hand stretched out
And the painful shoes
Forget the caveman age
And always raise the fist of the people
In the crackling of the underground fire

TRANSLATED BY BUBAKAR ADJALI

The Bomb and Time

(Nedjma was to remain standing, very close to the door,
the parcel on the floor by her feet, then pretend to
forget it in the excitement of the crowd and get off
immediately at the next stop. But now everything is
changed. . . . The travelers must remain seated and keep
their parcels on their lap. Nedjma remains impassive,
but her voice can be heard in a soft whisper, "It's my
turn today. I shall drag many with me. . . ." as she watches
the crowds of travelers. Screams and laughter of children.
Faces of mothers and old men. The Algerian landscape
moves across the screen. She turns her eyes away and seems
to see Marguerite for the first time.)

Nedjma
   Don't forget to get off

Marguerite
   I'll get off with you
(Pause: Nedjma holds Marguerite by the hand. Then their
voices alternate.)

Oh! That the time would pass
But what is time
if not a bomb delayed
delayed?

Mustapha
   The same bomb pulls us in, responsible and yet not
   guilty, and thrown back among the innocents, as
   monsters of clairvoyance.

Nedjma and Marguerite
   At last, it is removed like a blindfold
   Time, this lasting lie
   Time, time that kills
   Time, which till now killed us in silence
   Time, which has recovered its bloody rhythm
   Its gallop, its furor
   Time, this lasting lie

   (A fast tic-tac, covered by the two voices.)

Time has recovered its bloody rhythm
It no longer knows how to lie, it gallops on, runs down,
It will never be able to punctuate the message
which others, mutilated and dead, have transmitted to us

Mustapha
   Time, that was our ignorance
   In the eyes of those who struggle
   A false world is crumbling
   Already they are elsewhere
   Already they rest in peace in the secret dwelling
   Where all of time is engulfed
   Like a stone

with no price
and no lies
among the weeds of oblivion

Nedjma and Marguerite
Time, that was our ignorance
We came without knowing it,
Inseparable from the bomb

Mustapha
Hardly was she a militant
and the other a sympathiser
and here they are
here they are volunteers
and here they are volunteers of death

Nedjma and Marguerite
In truth, death is not our domain
We shall quickly pass this dark moment

Mustapha
It is through your eyes that the nation will see the light

Nedjma and Marguerite
Reduced to being but a living explosion
held up right in the heart of the enemy
our blood must light up and we must be set afire
so the spectators may be moved
and so that, in the world, eyes may be opened
Not on our remains, but upon the wounds of the
    survivors

TRANSLATED BY BUBAKAR ADJALI

FROM THE EAST

Kimathi, the settler is not uprooted
Are these not his footprints!
Ocol is not alone. Did you say
Independence? We bleed . . . We bleed

Prayer

Solomon Deressa

Make the flame flow and the fountain smoke
On an adamant floor a handful of sand I'll sow
Fragile pebbles to harvest come the season of dearth.
There is not much else to do
Don't you see, the castle's heroic gun-rest
Is as from today a favourite suicide spot.

Crystal images to skin ourselves on, O Lord.

Intersection

Sleepy at a perfectly ordinary intersection
Sympathising with the aborted dawn
I watch fat little men scurry to early work
Call them "fathers of poets for tomorrow"
Think my stand "the cross-road of life"
For no reason at all.

□ □ □

(But don't we know that the newness in New, like dew
is a repetition of jaded motion in unconfirmed extension?)
Eviscerate the lies of faded souvenirs

When fear of death, fear of loss
paralyse the freedom of the unknown path
and force us into paces of infernal circles,
the consolation of poetry in self-absorption
harmonic solace (the song added) cold-blooded pretention
that today shall always be yesterday . . .

And then, a thousand years later, flayed
among the hedges with the unnameable laid I
listening to the Lost One's off-shoot tinkle
against the August rays pouring through an error-colour bottle:

>   Love of my love
>   Spiral of my descent
>   Iris of my light
>   Rose of May
>
>   Inflammation of a raw Sunday
>   Shimmer of dawn moon
>   Wine of "iritised" noon
>   Breath of twilight rum
>   Charges of the crackling comb
>   Lay of heyday
> Hay day
>   Soul of night
>   Essence of my blight
>   Reason of endless fight
> Endless
>   Shall we sing you a song
>   A futile night long?
> Futile
>   Or go out on the sly
>   To cry
>   Wading Canadian Rye?
> And cry
>   Ashes of my first dawn
>   Season of crimson red
>   Rainy-haired bosoms bared

Bared
> Shall we invent names
> To suffocate old games?
Old games
> Where were you sown
> Ashes of the first dawn
> Begotten and thrown
> Where are you gone?

> Rose of May
> Twilight grey,
> I meant to catch you
> And chink you
> And thatch you
> In an African tukul
> And suffocate you
> Between the sharp tips
> Of the colliding drums
> And kiss the silent apex of slain tam-tams.

> Oh, Rose
> Rose of May . . .

Ring the Child Alive

His temper it is, he thought,
Though it's his mind he lost
Gathering waif-ends and shells
Combing a cold deserted beach
For a child a thousand years dead.

A child is a child alive or dead,
He told himself, and years don't count
So much as the colour of shells

They are foot-prints on the sand
And the ebb will wash them out
And if the flow falls stubbornly short
Why then we shall raise a cathedral
And with turquoise froth dot it with spirals
Even two or three if need be
And make bells of the shells
Turn the sea into a gong
To ring the child alive
Disturbing his innocent slumber
And then lull him back to sleep.

Why?

Time is her, time is you
why a red pencil
when lead will do

Why a sonorous laugh
when a sulky rebuff
is more like you?

Similitudes

Scrupulously as sin
the Winter of youth moves in
and Fall retreating takes force with it

Like a death emptied black-blue sky
cupped empty like ignored letter loops
like a self-wasting desert fire

In the white of darkness . . . burnt, burnt, burnt
check each momentary self against dull aches
sorrows before hurt, string smiles as beads,

Weep my mistress while you obliquely sit
(see the shard's giant teeth bleed cold)
so ritual candles, passions flicker out

Gasping against vertigo the dark male of solitude
evades your vein-grained eyes in prayer
lover-like force-mounting the fields

When crimson blazes of dusk envelop a hoary earth
despite solitude no matter how clays weep and bleed
the fallacy of alienage fits the hollow desire of an abandoned hive

Yet, the end is at hand
and we are on our way home
be it to other self-wasting fires

The self from other selves
will not be told apart, death from undeath
similitudes are handcuffed though we keep the secret silent.

TRANSLATED FROM THE AMHARIC

The Dry Well

      The old black woman was *illettrée* and the child was
only three. Since there were no johns he was having a heavenly
go at it right behind the house. The boa-constrictor (referred

to as ancestral by some) came out of the dry well that had been
dug several generations earlier. Perhaps in the days when the
land was first occupied by their people. The old woman had no
personal memories of those times.

The big lethargic black snake twitched treacherously.
The child watched it with fascination as a white-eyed chocolate
doll might watch a child.

The old woman came out. She was not fascinated at
all. She knew of these things. Gripping an old spade, she
almost broke the constrictor's textured black back as would an
Italian cutting spaghetti dead with a soup spoon.

Learning started that evening. All living things
were given meaning. The mysteries of Heaven and Earth were
disclosed. Among the lessons was this:

The sky used to be a real roof above our heads until
one day a mule with itchy hooves kicked it. And a God who had
more wit than humour raised the floor of his palace way out of
reach. The wages of accident being those of premeditation, the
mule became forever sterile. We, who had nothing to do with it,
got a better deal: the high, blue, clear African sky.

The leathery old woman, reclining on her checkered
leather bed, would have understood it all differently perhaps.
But then, it is hardly likely that she thought herself a black
woman. She had no information on other pigments.

▢ ▢ ▢

The names of you all
I loved and hurt
Hurt and burnt

I burnt
The source the glow flows from.
So, if I turn my head away
At the sight of books
Old shoes and fishing-hooks,
Sentimentality is incidental.
Flashes of freight-pain
Thaw through anti-climax-wise.

To stay the collision of worlds
And blurr the bleak precision of vision,
Although the harm is already done
I cork my ears against all your names

Turn me away blind if I forget a face.

The odds are against yesterday
Overflowing past
With wisdom for which no words found
To deafness entrusted
Humble petitioners dumb they must stand.

Crunching at chinks off a putrid wall
To bore a hole at my own height
Witness I become to enamel shorn and fall
And pulps into jaundice-poison flower.

Similar to senile chiliastic obsessions *semé*
Severed the arabesque of insulated connections,
Too late to haul back yesterday cut loose
Epiphenomena, unrelated float in simple suit.

The odds are against yesterday.

Foot-path

Stella Ngatho

Path-let . . . leaving home leading out
Return my mother to me,
Though you are wide or narrow
Return my mother to me.
The sun is sinking and darkness coming
Hens and cocks are already inside and babies drowsing,
Return my mother to me.
We do not have fire-wood and the hurricane lamp I have not seen.

There is no more food and the water has run out,
Path-let I pray you, Return my mother to me.
Path of the hillocks, Path of the small stones
Path of slipperiness, path of mud
Return my mother to me.
Path of the papyrus, path of the rivers
Path of the small forests, path of the reeds
Return my mother to me.
Path that winds, path of the short-cut;
Over-trodden path, newly made path,
Return my mother to me.
Path, I implore you, Return my mother to me.
Path of the crossways, path that branches off,
Path of the stinging shrubs, path of the bridge
Return my mother to me.
Path of the open path of the valley
Path of the steep climb, path sloping down
Return my mother to me.
Children are drowsing about to sleep,
Darkness is coming and there is no fire-wood,
And I have not found the hurricane lamp
Return my mother to me.

The Kraal

The kraal fence
        hides quarrels of jealous wives,
It hides the miseries within
        and sadness
of wives fallen from favour
It restricts anyone
        beyond its gate from inside
That reed fence
        spells laughter, joy
and happiness to the outside
        but hides the cruelty
of the husband within
            to the tortured tormented wife,
the sad one full of woes,
        the favoured one full of ease and joy
Yes, that reed fence hides plenty.

A Young Tree

Alone in the vast forest of elders
A young tree grows
Dreaming of days she'll be accepted
Surrounded by her silent mates
And beardy elders

She is gay and sad and happy, yet
Not knowing why.

Among the majesty of beardy elders
Wrapped in tottering beauty
Tinged with grey
Knowing for one and all
She never will be happy with her lot until
Her branches touch the blue.

Alone with her silent mates
Along among beardy elders
Her mind meanders across
Broody shadows of time growing old
Time arrested at dawn
Reaching out for peace
With the elders and time.

My Husband's House Is a Dark Forest of Books

Okot p'Bitek

Listen, my clansmen,
I cry over my husband
Whose head is lost.
Ocol has lost his head
In the forest of books.

When my husband
Was still wooing me
His eyes were still alive,
His ears were still unblocked,
Ocol had not yet become a fool
My friend was a man then!

He had not yet become a woman,
He was still a free man,
His heart was still his chief.

My husband was still a Black man
The son of the Bull
The son of Agik
The woman from Okol
Was still a man,
An Acoli.

My husband has read much,
He has read extensively and deeply,
He has read among white men
And he is clever like white men

And the reading
Has killed my man,
In the ways of his people

He has become
A stump.

He abuses all things Acoli,
He says
The ways of black people
Are black
Because his eyeballs have exploded,
And he wears dark glasses,

My husband's house
Is a dark forest of books.
Some stand there
Tall and huge
Like the *tido* tree

Some are old
Their barks are peeling off
And they smell strongly.
Some are thin and soft.

The backs of some books
Are hard like the rocky stem of the *poi* tree,
Some are green
Others red as blood
Some books are black and oily,
Their backs shine like
The dangerous *ororo* snake
Coiled on a tree top.

Some have pictures on their backs,
Dead faces of witch-looking men and women,
Unshaven, bold, fat-stomached
Bony-cheeked, angry revengeful-looking people,
Pictures of men and women
Who died long ago.

The papers on my husband's desk
Coil threateningly

Like the giant forest climbers,
Like the *kituba* tree
That squeezes other trees to death;
Some stand up,
Others lie on their backs,
They are interlocked
Like the legs of youths
At the *orak* dance,
Like the legs of the planks
Of the *goggo* fence,
They are tightly interlocked
Like the legs of the giant forest climbers
In the impenetrable forest

My husband's house
Is a mighty forest of books,
Dark it is and very damp,
The steam rising from the ground
Hot thick and poisonous
Mingles with the corrosive dew
And the rain drops
That have collected in the leaves.

They choke you
If you stay there long,
They ruin your nose and tongue
So that you can no longer
Enjoy the fresh smell of simsim oil
Or the taste of *malakwang*;

And the boiling darkness
Bursts your eye balls.
And the sticky juices
That drop from the gum trees
Block the holes of your ears,
And when ten girls
Standing on the hillock
In the moonlight

Sing *oyele* songs,
Throwing stones of abuse
At the rough-skinned ugly old men
Chosen for them as husbands
By their money-loving fathers,

Or when your daughter
Sings a lovely lullaby
To her baby brother
Strapped on her back,
And she sways forwards and backwards
As she sings

> *O baby*
> *Why do you cry?*
> *Are you ill?*
> *O baby stop crying*
> *Your mother has fried the* aluru *birds*
> *In ghee!*

When the girls sing *oyele* songs
And the nurse sings her lullaby
You hear only noises,
Noises that disturb you
Like a brick
Thrown on top of the iron roof.

If you stay
In my husband's house long,
The ghosts of the dead men
That people this dark forest,
The ghosts of the many white men
And white women
That scream whenever you touch any book,
The deadly vengeance ghosts
Of the writers
Will capture your head,

And like my husband
You will become
A walking corpse.

My husband's ears are numb,
He hears the crackling sounds
Of the gums within the holes of his ears
And thinks this is the music
Of his people;
He cannot hear
The insults of foreigners
Who say
The songs of black men are rubbish!

Listen, my husband,
Hear my cry!
You may not know this
You may not feel so,
But you behave like
A dog of the white man!
A good dog pleases its master,
It barks at night
And hunts in the salt lick
It chases away wild cats
That come to steal the chicken!
And when the master calls
It folds its tail between the legs.

The dogs of white men
Are well trained
And they understand English!

When the master is eating
They lie by the door
And keep guard
While waiting for left-overs.

But oh! Ocol
You are my master and husband,
You are the father of these children
You are a man,
You are you!

Do you not feel ashamed
Behaving like another man's dog
Before your own wife and children?

My husband, Ocol
You are a Prince
Of an ancient chiefdom,
Look,
There in the middle of the homestead
Stands your grandfather's Shrine,
Your grandfather was a Bull among men
And although he died long ago
His name still blows like a horn,
His name is still heard
Throughout the land.

When he died
Your father proudly
Built him that Shrine!
A true son of his father
He carried out all the duties
Of a first-born son.

He himself was a great chief
Well beloved by his people.
At the *otole* dance
He was right in the middle
Completely surrounded by his host
Like the termite queen mother,
But you could spot him
By his huge head-gear
Waving like a field of flowering sugar-cane.

In battle he fought at the front
Fierce like a wounded buffalo-girl,
When his men struck the enemy
The heaven shook from its base;

Has the Fire produced Ash?
Has the Bull died without a Head?
Aaa! A certain man
Has no millet field,
He lives on borrowed foods.
He borrows the clothes he wears
And the ideas in his head
And his actions and behaviour
Are to please somebody else.
Like a woman trying to please her husband!
My husband has become a woman!

Then why do you wear a shirt?
Why do you not tie
A sheet round your waist
As other women do?
Put on the string skirt
And some beads on your loins!

★

O, my clansmen,
Let us all cry together!
Come,
Let us mourn the death of my husband,
The death of a Prince
The Ash that was produced
By a great Fire!
O, this homestead is utterly dead,
Close the gates
With *lacari* thorns,
For the Prince
The heir to the Stool is lost!

And all the young men
Have perished in the wilderness!
And the fame of this homestead
That once blazed like a wild fire
In a moonless night
Is now like the last breaths
Of a dying old man!

There is not one single true son left,
The entire village
Has fallen into the hands
Of war captives and slaves!
Perhaps one of our boys
Escaped with his life!
Perhaps he is hiding in the bush
Waiting for the sun to set!

But will he come
Before the next mourning?
Will he arrive in time?

Bile burns my inside!
I feel like vomiting!

For all our young men
Were finished in the forest,
Their manhood was finished
In the class-rooms,
Their testicles
Were smashed
With large books!

FROM THE SOUTH

There are words here,
As any place. Desire
& reality with the stench
& brutality of a blunt knife
against a gumful of pus

Letters to Martha

Dennis Brutus

1

After the sentence
mingled feelings:
sick relief,
the load of the approaching days
apprehension—
the hints of brutality
have a depth of personal meaning;

exultation—
the sense of challenge
of confrontation,
vague heroism
mixed with self-pity
and tempered by the knowledge of those
who endure much more
and endure . . .

2

One learns quite soon
that nails and screws
and other sizeable bits of metal
must be handed in;

and seeing them shaped and sharpened
one is chilled, appalled
to see how vicious it can be
—this simple, useful bit of steel:

and when these knives suddenly flash
—produced perhaps from some disciplined anus—
one grasps at once the steel-bright horror
in the morning air
and how soft and vulnerable is naked flesh.

6

Two men I knew specifically
among many cases:
their reactions were enormously different
but a tense thought lay at the bottom of each
and for both there was danger and fear and pain—
drama.

One simply gave up smoking
knowing he could be bribed
and hedged his mind with romantic fantasies
of beautiful marriageable daughters;

the other sought escape
in fainting fits and asthmas
and finally fled into insanity:

so great the pressures to enforce sodomy.

7

Perhaps most terrible are those who beg for it,
who beg for sexual assault.

To what desperate limits are they driven
and what fierce agonies they have endured
that this, which they have resisted,
should seem to them preferable,
even desirable.

It is regarded as the depths
of absolute and ludicrous submission.
And so perhaps it is.

But it has seemed to me
one of the most terrible
most rendingly pathetic
of all a prisoner's predicaments.

9

The not-knowing
is perhaps the worst part of the agony
for those outside;

not knowing what cruelties must be endured
what indignities the sensitive spirit must face
what wounds the mind can be made to inflict on itself;

and the hunger to be thought of
to be remembered
and to reach across space
with filaments of tenderness
and consolation.

And knowledge,
even when it is knowledge of ugliness
seems to be preferable,
can be better endured.

And so,
for your consolation
I send these fragments,
random pebbles I pick up
from the landscape of my own experience,
traversing the same arid wastes
in a montage of glimpses
I allow myself
or stumble across.

11

Events have a fresh dimension
for all things can affect the pace
of political development—

but our concern
is how they hasten or delay
a special freedom—
that of those the prisons hold
and who depend on change
to give them liberty.

And so one comes to a callousness,
a savage ruthlessness—
voices shouting in the heart
"Destroy! Destroy!"
or
"Let them die in thousands!"—

really it is impatience.

    11 *November* 1965

14

How fortunate we were
not to have been exposed
to rhetoric

—it would have falsified
a simple experience;
living grimly,
grimly enduring

Oh there was occasional heroic posturing
mainly from the immature
—and a dash of demagogic bloodthirstiness

But generally
we were simply prisoners
of a system we had fought
and still opposed.

Presumably
one should pity the frightened ones
the old fighters
who now shrink from contact:
and it is true I feel a measure of sadness
—and no contempt—
and have no wish to condemn
or even grow impatient

But it is best to shutter the mind and heart
eyes, mouth and spirit;
say nothing, feel nothing and do not let them know
    that they have cause for shame

Sacrilege to Self

Zweli ed Dladla

                love thy neighbor
The white world spits in my face.
                turn the other cheek
They don't slap the other cheek.
They wring my soul out of me.
And this is the world I'm born in.
                thou shalt not kill
Mother brother father sister fall by my side.
They did not kill, no.
Mercy-killing is no kill.
Is it possible to kill a killed one.
Once you kill and the second time around is mercy-killing.
                infinite mercy!
I'm a believer.
                trust the lord
I pour the whole of me to the lord.
And my trust don't reach him nowhere.
Seasonal winds blow that trust off his reach.
Piratic winds loot my trust.
And the myopic trust stay locked in the harem of white mistletoes.
What price to pay?
What ransom?
                repent.
Self-murder I'll inflict.
To die for the folly of trust.
To die for the betrayal of self.
To die for the resurrection of fallen kin.
To die for life.
To die for love.
To die to live.
                and fuck the lord.

Dribbling Around

With muzzles of our guns
pointed to our mouths.
We rattle and rattle
chewing stones to gravel with our teeth.
Tis no heavy chore.
Tis just false choice.
Choosing ecstatic death with borrowed guns
that point nowhere
but ourselves.
We dribble around
taking tools of death from the makers of our death.
While spouting anger in falsetto voices
that shy away into ruffle sounds of green papers.
Dribble around we do.
Maiming hope for those who check lives and life from between
trapped pages.

A Song of Hope

Tis not agony that brings tears to my eyes.
Tears painful tears.
Tears impotent tears.
Tis not pity that curls lumps in my throat.
Lumps convulsing lumps.
Lumps excruciating lumps.

Neither is it joy,
Joy futile joy.
My heart knows not joy.
Frozen hearts know no joy.
Frozen souls no ecstasy.
Frozen souls no pain.
Frozen souls no pity.
Frozen souls no feel.

Slaved by empty promises.
Snared in vague assurances.
The feel is bottled.
The feel is numbed.
The feel is rendered insensible.

Tis the hope that cries me.
Hope unfutile hope.
Hope tangible hope.
Hope in action.
Active action.
Deathwise action.
Deathwise to living.
Living a dream.
A nostalgic dream.
Dream of an elusive value.
A dispossessed value.
Wrenched from the souls, hearty black souls,
that lie nurturing the soil.
Dead.
Dead for a value.
Freedom.

Inertia

there's silence in the room
blue silence as in a skyless day
blue and heavy
pounding
staring
ominous
cheerless as a brittle newborn baby trapped in a wintry sewage
it laughs
wicked and hollow
the silence laughs deafening
this side and this
the other side
no
no side
everywhere
the silence and the forms vacant
impotent eyes rolling colorlessly red in insane orbits toward
fleeting forms of sterile stupors
a dull thudding with no sound persists
silence
gray as death
gray and fierce as a rainless cloud hovering above the skies
silence
humid
stifling
crushing.
Burst! Burst! Burst!
Flow out as pus . . . bloody pus . . .
Leperous wounds smarting, spew the shit!

oh
there's silence in the room
blue silence as in a skyless day
blue and heavy
pounding
staring
ominous

Epitaph on Faces

I cannot remember you my brother.
Perhaps it is the snow in your eyes.
Let me wipe the cold in your death-eyes . . .
or your lips are sordid from the penny-songs you seem to sing.

I cannot hear your voice.
It shines beyond the cackle of queen jezebel who fed the peasants
with caviar and pumpkin-seeds when they discovered the corn
stuffed in her bloomers under her pillow.

"Twas a noble gesture" remarked the albino who counted dimes
under his tongue while winking at the sun.

For a while I thought I knew you my brother.
Let's chant mayibuye/comeback together thus walking back to
the future we forgot.
Or, is your voice brassed by the golden handles of your coffin?

Perhaps I can reach you from below here.
Kings are buried in/with their knapsacks you know.
Will that hinder your hand from holding mine?

I cannot remember you my brother.
Kaffirboy and niggerboy are dying too.
Will that sound too sad for you?

I was told at the morgue it was about time.
But somehow I have suspicions they are masquerading as you.
What a lonesome death they should die in souls and bodies
not their own.
Or perhaps I didn't know you my brother.

The streets and the shanties were your camouflage.
But I cannot believe in reincarnation if the führer and voster
are to come as du pont merged in your body.
But again my mind is burned to ashen butterflies.
Let me remember you my brother not in the bondage we all
   shunned.

II.

Resurrection is no jew monopoly/or juju for those to die.

I can hear you still.
Your fury shrill in the melody of your penny-whistle,
shrieking beautiful obscenities in the corners of eloff
to the delight of your unlistening audience who toss dimes
and pennies at your feet while you wail and sing, niggerboy
niggerboy, kaffirboy kaffirboy, till when?

It Happened

We held so long on dead rites.
Our minds dying in our face.
We held much too long.
Dreaming of death rites on mainstreams.
Mainstreams flowing to sewages of our souls.
Much too long we held.
Every breadth of our life
a gasp to breathe death from openings

openings that open to carrion streams
that wash holding hands away.
Much too long we held.

The Wilderness

Now I walk the wilderness, the curse of Qamata ringing hysteria
    to my waywardness.
I watch myself steadily straddling two collapsing worlds.
My right foot on a death-ride to nowhereness.
My left foot on a world torn apart by people whose meaning is
    death.
And I see my groin torn asunder as the worlds collapse, with my
    feet astride on both.
I have no horror for the void all things will be thrown in.
It is a numbness no death-words could begin to aptly formulate.
Bygod! it is a bleakness no insights can begin to fathom.
It is a terror the wrath of Qamata could have hardly foreseen.
Blind rage at the callous neglect of orderings.
The curse on me!
I cannot begin to want to look back to the hysteric moment of
    Somandla,
Maker of all things in my life,
When he banished me to the lowliest loneliness and impotence
When in a spell of frivolous ignorance I turned my back on him.
It was a moment carefree and frivolous
When like a prostitute I spread-opened my skull to poisonous
    darts that turned me to a lack-lustre effigy of humanity.
Qamata was angry, and rightly so.
His anger beyond control
Resounded thru all the corners of my motherland; thru all the
    corners of the continent of the dark.

Lakes dried and mountains crumbled.

Trees withered and birds stopped their song.

Cattle lay dying on all fields and black breasts and black wombs
atrophied.

Fetal aberrations took the order of the day.

The land was death.

And I had no alibi for existence.

And all the living in it were sprawled limbs of a maimed corpse
after the ejaculations of a necrophiliac who came clutching a
book in one hand and jingling coins in the other.

All the mothers no longer were mothers.

The black sperm had coagulated to greyish pus.

And everybody whored their lives in every direction.

It's not a land for pity.

It's not a land of misery.

It's not a land of sadness.

It is a land of ashen sterility peopled by crude mimics of life.

It is a mammoth of graveyards where death is the greeting and
salutation of the day.

Each dying phantom says, "Death," and in kind the other replies,
"Death."

And silently fall on the wayside to die.

Qamata was angry, and rightly so.

He banished false life and vanished to wander in agony beyond
the reach of the dead.

No blood for solace.

No libations.

And the world is powder dry; everything, powder dry.

It used to have a name, but I don't know its name.

All the ancestors scurried in fright to decorated tombs,

And hid beneath engraved marble stones.

False calls of theatricality might perhaps make them peep.

But no contact with Qamata.

No mediation.

They, too, died the deserving death of all the pretenders to life
with all their false prophesies of a new world to come.

Worlds are collapsing in all directions.

And all the riders are falling in.

The visual horror of what is to come is hidden from their
encapsulated perceptions.

Perception they have alright,

But it is contorted and polluted by the desires to cheat themselves
into believing that they exist,

Whilst theirs is nothing but a death ride from one death to
another.

Qamata! Somandla! Open our eyes!

But alas these are nothing but false alarms

Designed and dedicated to the dramatization of a loss no one
has nobody to deceive and to blame but himself.

I know the curse is on me.

And I have to harness it;

To bridle it.

But I lost control a million years before death and I know I can
reclaim it.

Qamata is not dead.

He never died.

And will never die.

No bleary and pretentious images on sidewalks will conjure up his
concealed whereabouts.

And all conjurers and jugglers will fall flat on their faces in
alchemic attempts to trap him with their words.

His revelation will come as self-revelation unfolds itself to each and
everyone.

Qamata is not a god.

Qamata is not God.

Qamata is Anger.

An all-purpose anger to kick yourself and wake up to your death.

And all narcissists of anger do nothing but kick the mirrors of
their death

And shatter them only to deceive themselves into believing that
they have mustered genuine anger to lift themselves from
their ghastly deaths.

But death rides,
A virus in the mouths of pretenders to anger;
Molded anger,
Dramatic,
Theatric,
An insidious and vitriolic balm to all those who look up to the
    polemic transvestites for guidance.
All, all is slave-paranoia.
A creation of the children of the wilderness
Who like their tongues in the asses of their masters.

New York, New York
December 1970

Land of the Lull

Deep in the barbarous south lands sore heads in unison banged.
A resounding rhythm echoed
piercing the proud hearts of the relics of a proud people.

Far in the marooned south keen murmurs in harmony rose.
A purposeful hope formed
resurrecting the moribund hopes of a trodden people.

The murmur, the rhythm, the violent melody
charmed the native ear and shied other ears.
In gleeful appreciation one stomped his feet.
In fearful apprehension the other coiled his feet,
to spring in vengeful retaliation; to clip the rhythm of violence.

Now deep in the south lands all is in a tense hush.
Banging heads, moving murmurs stay hushed by harsh sounds of
    cannons.

No mimicry of the robust spirit of the sounds is heard.
A lull looms, punctuated in staccatos by chordless whines
as moans of a wounded fox.
No thud of the rhythmic stomps vibrates with violence.
Feeble feet fall faint like flies on a winter dead dog.

The feeble feign, wriggle and squirm.
Wriggling wretchedly in abandon of the rhythm of violence.
Squirming miserably in denial of the song of violence.
Cringing like car-crushed dogs toward their masters.
Betraying the sacred sounds of the bang
the murmur
the rhythm
the violence.

Origins

Keorapetse Kgositsile

deep in your cheeks
your specific laughter owns
all things south of the ghosts
we once were. straight ahead
the memory beckons from the future
You and I a tribe of colors
this song that dance
godlike rhythms to birth
footsteps of memory
the very soul aspires to. songs
of origins songs of constant beginnings
what is this thing called
love

Tropics

Forever beginning
Forever laughing
And more laughter transpierced
By the birth of new eyes
Striding from petrified ice
To smoking stone to stone
Like bleeding memories
Of childbirth it is.
How deny that man can
Be born in the womb of a woman
Other than the overseas mother
Nursing his memories

Into upright method
Transpiercing western native township dooms?
They dubbed the township western
They did not know their irony
Here now beside the woman's face
Forever beginning
From ice to sunlit bush
Forever laughing

For Melba

Morning smiles
In your eye
Like a coy moment
Captured by an eternal
Noon and from yesterdays
I emerge naked
Like a Kimberley diamond
Full like Limpopo after rain
Singing your unnumbered charms

For Ipeleng

(dedicated to Gerry T & the students who unleashed it at Bennett)

I saw her come here with no words,
arms flailing air, past mother, thigh,
and blood. Here we begin again

We shall know each other
by the root of our appetite

or rhythm; Big Mama Juicy
Aneb seemed to say.
Her eye direct as comment. As
roaches or rats. As heads cracked
open for fun or law&order
in this strange place

When I woke up one morning
I saw her coming in the stillness
of her day and want. My eye sprung out
to embrace a season of dreams.
But she asked: if mother or father
is more than parent, is this my land
or merely soil to cover my bones?

To Mother

Toward the laughter we no longer
know; this way we must from now
on and always, past shapes
turned into shadows of wish
and want, regret too. Your
eye, I know, is stronger than faith in
some god who never spoke our language.

And there it seems to have been aborted.
Words, and they are old and impotent. Here
a slave will know no dance of laughter.

What of the act my eye demands
past any pretentious power of any word
I've known? My days have fallen
into nightmarish despair. I know
no days that move on toward laughter,

except in memory stale as our glory.
I see no touch of determined desire
past the impotence of militant rhetoric.
The anguished twists of our crippled day will not
claim my voice. Woman dancer-of-steel,
did you ever know that the articulate silence
of your eye possessed my breath for long days?
Yet still I know no dance but the slow
death of a dazed continent.
We claim the soil of our home
runs in our blood yet we run
around the world, the shit of others
drooling over our eye. We know
no dance in our blood now but doom.
So who are the newlyborn
who, unquestionable,
can claim the hands of the son?

For Eusi, Ayi Kwei & Gwen Brooks

In us and into us and ours
This movement rises every day
As the day whose fire informs
The rhythm of the sons who must live
After the death of those familiar faces

We move from origin,
The singular fruit, at times bitter
As the Sophiatown winters we did not create,
To roots, stronger than the grief
Which groans under the weighted
Centuries of systematic rape and ruin

We move from origin to roots.
Past the rancid face of anger and sorrow
Where I was a stranger to my breath
Rests the color of my eye
Calling my name
In the depths that reclaim
My pulse in the darknesses that alone
Remember the face of the warrior
Whose name knows a multiple doom
Before he is born to follow the eye
To the shapes remembered where the spirit moves
On to the darknesses the eye caresses
In us and into us and ours

The New Breed

(for don lee & mazisi kunene)

And generations still come or go
Mine, born deaf, never learned
The power of fire.
                    See how they run
Around the world on their knees!
Still you must wheel, bird of long reach
Move in the air with air
Out there. We are unleashed voices
And millions of hands to mold
What then is life, livable.

And breath is our hands
To caress breasts of fire
Which then is living, lovable.
Swing, blood of new breed, swing

Or do the dance of fire, thundering
In city or jungle with the newly born
Lancing whatever vein keeps poisoning
The body of the eye of your generation

Anthem of Decades (Extract from an epic)

Mazisi Kunene

Part I

And then time was born:
The millepede-darkness encircled the earth
And silence surged into space like a pregnant moon.
Tufts of darkness entangled in the horizon
Making the earth heave like a giant heart.
The crooked mountains await the first fruit of the sun.
Whilst the night triumphed, the stars thrust their swords of light,

(Which, the tale goes, were worlds older than ours)
Tearing the black blanket with its hidden mysteries.
The creator who created heaven and earth
Filled this planet with the commotion of beasts
And walked the great path of the skies,
Looking on the hungry chasms of the mountains,
The racing of great rivers and spacious oceans
Whose waves beat eternally on the vast shores.

The belly of the earth split open
Releasing animals that crawl on the earth
And others that fly with their wings
And others that drum their hoofs on the ground.
The lion roared thundering the first fear.
Other beasts less ferocious stared
Until, aware of the satisfying taste of blood,
Joined in the general carnage.
So the lesson was learnt. Life must continue
And good things must feed the ruthlessness of appetites.

At the beginning the creator had messengers
Whom he sent to the ends of the universe:
Sodume, the Intelligence of Heaven,

Who explored the labyrinths of the earth
And opened the gates to all the creatures that inhabit the earth.

Satisfied with this work
He sang as they paraded
"These multitudes will fill this world of stone
The forests will be stampeding with wild animals
The mountains will be gambolling with antelopes
The overflowing rivers will be pregnant with life.
But in all this man is yet to come,
Proud and defiant before all things."
So over and over he repeated the ecstasy of heaven
Like him who sings alone the anthems of life.

There was Simo who stood guard
At the limits of the universe,
Who blotted out, at intervals, the light of the moon
And darkness would return to the earth hoping to regain its lost
    territory.
He travelled often accompanied by the children of Sodume.
The wild ones who loved best
To flash the forks of lightning.
Their father Sodume lived near the earth
Where he played games with his wife Nodume.
She screamed, echoing her voice across the path of the sky.
But Sodume's voice, round and powerful, shook the heavens.
Often he emerged with her in relentless pursuit.
Both cherished the bluebird of heaven
Whose tail was deep blue, whose wings were blue
Whose body was blue but whose feet were of burning red.
Wherever they were they let it fly before them like a cloud.

Sometimes it would spread its wings descending on the earth
And tearing firm mountains from their roots.
Those who know say even its lungs spit fire
Whose great flames shatter the earth
So that in the minds of all
It symbolised the wrath of the gods.

In all this the power of the creator
Revealed itself in his daughter, the princess of life,
  Nomkhubulwane.
She was the source of all life.
She gave abundance to the hungry of the earth.
For this even animals hailed her in their worlds
And gambolled like young calves at play.
The princess of life was loved for her songs,
Whoever heard them would lie down
Repeating their music over and over again in his heart.
Even on this day of august debates
They all listened as she touched on the unknown and beautiful
  themes,
Saying: "We have fulfilled the other tasks of creation
But they are not complete without man,
He who will bind all things of existence,
A great shepherd who excels with wisdom."
She did not indulge in long endless debates
Since even those who listened to her took long to understand
As on the day of creation they did not understand.
But Somazwi dreaded by all, who speaks with the vehemence of
  fire
Did not wait long, like all who are poised with suspicion
Terrified of the power that challenges them in their glory,
They who follow all new ideas with the violence of their eyes.
He replied like one whose words burn the lips
And said: "Here begins again the old tale of blunders
As when long ago we remonstrated in the wind
Saying it is enough that our great assembly exists,
We, the ultimate expression of the power of the creator.
But now we hear this strange story of a new power
That will supervise all things with knowledge."
He spoke as they all listened with extended ears
Knowing that though they did not hold affection for him
His mind was as swift as the horn of a bull.

His followers clustered together like a brood,
As always, applauding each word he put forward.
Others delighted in the clash of words
Saying let the giants show their strength.
They waited for Sodume,
Whose intelligence baffled those known for their wisdom
As if even the winds listened when he spoke.
Somazwi continued: "What will this creature
Do with knowledge that excels all created things
Endowed as they are with enough for each day.
On the next day they still have enough for their daily needs
But I fear that this creature on knowing so much
Will experience the pains of yesterday and the unfulfilled
    tomorrow.
When it realises the defects of its clan
It will build dreams that will never be fulfilled
And wander everywhere with painful doubts asking the question
'What is the earth, of what value is life?'
It will not be enough to revel in the beauties of an earthly life."
He spoke so wisely that even those who supported
    Nomkhubulwane
Began to doubt and were swayed by Somazwi's thoughts.
All shook in their seats with questions.
Sodume alone listened
As if inspired by visions others could not reach.
He turned to his wife who rested her hand on his shoulder
Saying: "The life we live deprives us of wisdom,
We are overwhelmed by things before us."
Scarcely had he finished these words when someone stood
Turning to him as if he heard him:
"Great fighter who overwhelms with fierce powers
Do not allow the fire of words to burn beautiful things
As if these words were the very kernel of truth.
Unsheath your thoughts and cut these poisonous doubts
Of even those who have been swayed.
We all know a great path leads forward.

In it, all solutions evolve.
You, with only a few words, can straighten crooked thoughts."
He was silent and so were all the others.
It was as if whoever spoke first would create great conflagrations.
Sodume did not respond.
He listened like all wise men
Who do not rush without untying each knot.
Sometimes when they discover the truth they only laugh in their
    hearts
Knowing how words are like seeds
Which fall from the hands in their hundreds, most dying in their
    shells.
One who was known for his love of pleasure stood up
And thought he might speak.
So that they may remember pots frothing with beer
He said: "How can we solve in a day such great mysteries
We must settle down under the shade delving into the truth."
Others stared at each other pleased with these words
But none was eager to be seen filled with enthusiasm
Since there must be no talk of hunger in great assemblies.
Opponents continued to talk fiercely
Saying: "The creation of man is no desire of the creator,"
It seemed those who opposed the creation of man would triumph
Bidding with their words saying:
"This foolish creature will walk blindly, knowing and yet not
    knowing.
Since a pleasant life must define its boundaries."

After a long debate
Nomkhubulwane was heard asking for their attention.
She called over and over again as she had provoked the debate.
As she stood up the sun shook with her shadow
Addressing him who favoured beasts to man,
She said: "These arguments of the day have strange forebodings.
Those who oppose the hand of creation
Do so believing that what is, is complete.

But they do not understand, creation must always create.
Its essence is its change.
From it abundance splits itself to make abundance.
Whoever loves its greatness does not question it
Since to question is to weave strange tangles.
Its greatness is its expanse as always.
Somazwi and all those who are swept by his words do not know
That this creature, man, shall derive his power
From the very struggle of incomplete power
Which alone will rouse his mind with the appetite of wisdom."
She spoke these words knowing what lay hidden in their fears.
Even now the truth of what was to come formed itself within
    them.
They all listened, even the excitable followers of Somazwi
Since they still held her high in their esteem not for prestige,
But for her thoughts that burn like a thin sword.
He who had long depended on wisdom for his fame called out.
As he began to talk they all turned their eyes
Guessing what wisdom Sodume was to unravel.
"I have listened to the skilful tongues
Saying what value will it be to man
That he should walk in ignorance, blind of his fate.
But such questions and remarks have their weaknesses.
Whoever is the umbilical cord of life denies his existence
If he disputes the oneness of which he is extension.
It is not he alone who is, who is the reality of creation,
But those who are and others who shall be
Since the eye of life extends to the vastness of eternity.
The daughter of heaven has spoken all truths.
Whoever has not heard
Harbours his own kind of truth which he shall not reveal before
    us."
The great gathering listened,
Each trying to untie the profound meanings in Sodume's words.
Others questioned these thoughts saying truth is always relative
But others could not reach conclusions,

Their faces rigid with amazement.
Sodume continued: "The mind is the essence of conquest.
If man is endowed with this power
Even lions who boast their strength will fear him.
I and others who love the extension of life
Say let men stand supreme over the earth."

The chorus of those who agreed echoed
And as was customary a great anthem was heard
A eulogy from those who favoured mankind.
Someone from the assembly shouted:
"It is ours, this voice, it is ours."
When this mysterious debate was over, they all dispersed in their
  ways.
There were great feasts at the house of Somahle
Who was the source of all pleasure;
Whoever entered this house revelled as he wished.
A great hubbub was heard as they laughed and drank.
Some held beer pots decorated with stars
Some mocked others saying: "You were silent, great talker"
Addressing him who never spoke but always listened.
Sodume threw a ball of fire
Displaying flashes of lightning in the distant horizon
Its flashes making paths in the sky
Those who like to play sped down on them
Swinging from ray to ray as they descended to the earth.

The Gold-miners

Towers rise to the skies,
Sounds echo their music,
Bells ring backwards and forwards

Awakening the crowds from the centre of fire.
Attendants at the feast glitter,
Wealth piles on the mountains.
But where are the people?
We stand by watching the parades
Walking the deserted halls
We who are locked in the pits of gold.

Puzzle, or Man the Despicable Animal

One, I have kept great loves
Two, but few desired them
Three, the few were greedy ones
Four, how I hated them!

Therefore I have let this great love
Decay at the sacred place.
One day
The rats will emerge bloated with the feast
And celebrate the conquest of the earth.

They will give birth to men
Who will dance with the violence of thunder,
Proud of the maternity of rats,
Kindred with all ugliness.

Continuity

May it be so:
Let the great vessel be lifted from the ground
And the warm lips drink from it
Until the tongue begins to speak,
And spreads its song.
When thirst burns the mind
May we return again to the villages
Where we shall partake in a feast
With those that are no more.

Dedication

When you have crossed the river
Search for a fertile place.
There prepare the ground
And plant the seeds of our desire.
Plant it for the generations of summer
Who when they arrive will reap the harvest
And be filled with our fruit.
They will remember us in their tales
Saying this pleasure is mine and Ndondoshiya's
Meaning him and a thousand years.

People

As I live so do you live,
Because you are part of my existence.
If I inherited you with my knowledge
Then I would possess an ever-living ancestral spirit
Bound to other worlds.
When I have severed the umbilical cord
I still recognise the burial ground,
Since this essence echoes my experience.
Likewise the multitudes of my multitudes
Are the multiples of those that have known,
And bequeath the particles of their existence.

Friends

Honey are the words you speak
Whilst I drift slowly into sleep.
You tell the story over and over again.
I drowse in the palm of your hand
Whilst you hold the body aching with pain.
Softly you cover it
And whisper in my ear.
Although knowing I do not hear you,
You do it for the heart
Which alone never sleeps.

Thought on June 26

Was I wrong when I thought
All shall be avenged?
Was I wrong when I thought
The rope of iron holding the neck of young bulls
Shall be avenged?
Was I wrong
When I thought the orphans of sulphur
Shall rise from the ocean?
Was I depraved when I thought there need not be love,
There need not be forgiveness, there need not be progress,
There need not be goodness on the earth,
There need not be towns of skeletons,
Sending messages of elephants to the moon?
Was I wrong to laugh asphyxiated ecstasy
When the sea rose like quicklime
When the ashes on ashes were blown by the wind
When the infant sword was left alone on the hill top?
Was I wrong to erect monuments of blood?
Was I wrong to avenge the pillage of Caesar?
Was I wrong? Was I wrong?
Was I wrong to ignite the earth
And dance above the stars
Watching Europe burn with its civilisation of fire,
Watching America disintegrate with its gods of steel,
Watching the persecutors of mankind turn into dust
Was I wrong? Was I wrong?

Ode to Little Johnny's Dream

Burns B. Machobane

Mama . . .
One dese days 'am gonna
  Git me a ed'cation
  Be a Cong Guessman
  Make me lots a'money
  And
Guess what, Mama . . .
  Ah'ma marry me a
  White un.
Lawd!
Son,
  Y'alright!
All dat jist to
  git a white waman!

December 30, 1969

False Brothers

Rap to 'em, brother
Tell 'em about the man
Tell 'em to git together
      United we stand
      Divided we fall

Rap to 'em
Tell 'em about Af'ica

Black is beautiful
>They got to be hip
>They got to be wise

Y'also gonna tell 'em
That Tarzan's Ole Lady
Is also your Broad
Or are you . . . still . . .
Just usin' 'em . . . Brother
>Rap to me!

Lament

>After a sister had invited me to visit her
>where she lives with her white boy friend

When time was born,
Abyssinia was bare.
That's when the Nile sprang
That I might therefore spring
From the loins of Abyssinia.

When time was born,
When the Nile had sprung,
A serpent also sprang—
Though an age after I was born
Into the loins of Abyssinia

Should I forgive or forget?
Should I revenge or avenge?

>Shame!

July 20, 1970

FROM THE CENTER

Lumumba, do you hear us?
Our Home is not our home
The young will try to sing
What songs will move us from the season of death

Ife Head

Guy C. Z. Mhone

Why an ancestral nakedness
Thus exposed to them
Who spat on us
When you lay treasured in our soil
Below layers of generations
Of our dead.

Ife head, you stand there
Stone mute
Stripped and bare
No drums to beat
No tales to share
Mere stares of lust
Mediocre flattery at your past
They bestow on you

Here your tale we know
Hidden in the pen of our song
The communion of our feet/
                with our dark soil
Our twitches of the muscle/
                to tales of the drum
With you undug/
                your nakedness unexposed
Ife head
Why an ancestral nakedness
Thus exposed to them.

We rejoice now that they are dead. We
now shift our aristocratic asses and
bourgeois behinds well ensconced (albeit
temporarily) in the niches of foregone terrains. From
unseen horizons. '59–64, a mythical interlude
lost in Kamuzuan jingoism and do-it-yourself
history. Malawi a lovely toy of scattered Kamuzuan
palaces and barefoot marginal peasants.
"Malawians," accommodationist chickenshits
appropriately drilled to drool and
rejoice when Yatu is shot. Where are the
Malawians we used to be and used to know.
Not all could have succumbed to Pavlovian
sado-masochistic experimentalists like
. . . eh . . . like er . . . oh shit, forget it—

The Old Lady

She sits across us everyday
Her thoughts like tired fingers
Settle on familiar melodies of the past
Reminiscing lost years of old-fashionedness
And all the world
Seems funny
Plain funny

For death's melody is stale
Her thoughts by-pass it
Death's message is redundant
For she died on that day
The world looked funny

So now she sits
In an armchair of oblivion
Enveloped in a secure coffin
Of past familiar melodies.

A Lament to My Mother

I was sung to you
In me your first born
And now I see on my face
A wrinkle like your dimple
On your elbow/and now
Here I stand sinking in my dirt
But still the reason for your dimple
I will remember/black mother/
You cried me on a wrinkleless, black face
And bore a dimple on your elbow
Even though the spirals in your hair
Moistened by your silent tears
I still cannot see in the morning,
Black mother, I still am
One of the soil.

The Song of Nagondwe

See them stare at me
See them stare,
They stare
They stare and stare at me
At me
At me daughter of Mataka
Mataka,
Mataka of song and dance
And dance
and by dance Mataka lived
He lived
He lived and was soon to die
To die
To die beside his drum
His drum
His drum for which he named
He named, Potoko, Potoko, Ti Bata Bata.

Plucks guitar strings
And sings a lonely mind
In tune to life.

A life's song
So sweet from above
Riding happily

When underneath though
Bass notes knot out
Slender thoughts to sadness.

The Chisiza's I

Promoted, kicked upstairs
To a nowhere somewhere
We celebrated, rejoiced.
And now back
To a transcendental
Nowhere
They celebrate, rejoice

Rejoice?
We called them Du, Yatu,
Rejoice?
Dear God!
Or maybe, is it
Compromising timidity
Of a beleaguered peasantry.

Like time's timelessness
Our ancestors' agelessness
Du and Yatu live
In one with us,
Haunting the living
With an ancestral message
"HE must go"
Purgatorio? Inferno?

It behooves us
Yah, to do
What Yatu, Du
Craved for.

The Chisiza's II

They called him,
The Messiah
Within their fallibility,
Vulnerability,
Human confines of
Non-existent foresight

The Messiah
An embryonic Machiavellian "deliverer"
Then a potential form
Contradicting teleological existence.
To end, destroyed
In a Kafkaesque dilemma.

One a police Rhumba
One a Trade Union Kwela
They both did.
Existential placations abandoned,
Not for an amorphous cosmic realization,
But to actualise a people
Malawians.

They did it—
But were not done
The Symposium,
"Africa What Lies Ahead?"
But of a head, Du was dead.

The Messiah actualised,
Yatu Rhumba-ed away.
Existential Ndiche-ic pulsations

Called him back
To the nihilistic "deliverers" haven
And Yatu was dead.
"Africa what lies ahead?"
          dear god!

A Child of War: Biafra

They say there is a war, and now
My head is oversized and sits precariously
On my slender neck
Like a shrunken body of frozen passions.

My skin afraid to molt a cherished texture
Clings savagely and helplessly
To a useless skeletal artifice of patriotic bone
Like a sage to his divination
For my flesh has been sucked
Into existential negations
And all filiations desecrated
To utter forlornness.

My flesh, my life's cushion
Has smouldered in ideological furnaces
And my jugged bones
Pierce through the skin of my life
I can't even stand
For my life force is incarnated in war
It even hurts to live as a child
In such a filial absurdity
Of man and child, God and man.

I sat by the sun brooding
Far out on the Western fringe
Where numbers fade
And days transform

And there on tomorrow's clouds
I carved, from the East, a shadowy me
Which walked through me
And emerged in the West splintered
Into faded mes of yesterday

I saw it and I cried
I cried watery memories which
Flooded my hollow life
And those dopey mes
Smudging immaculate yesterdays
Kept on bobbing to the surface
Splashing contagious consciences
All over my consciousness

And I cried again
I cried a solaceless dream
And through my blood-shot eyes
I saw my soul!
It was there in the West
Happily kicking about my splintered mes
In yesterday's foggy field
Then it walked through me
(A perforated membrane I was)
And on to the East

Gaily chatting with the me I had carved
On those rainy clouds of tomorrow
Yes that was my soul
Just a spritely continuum

And then I awoke
Still sitting by the sun
On that far out Western fringe
And still searching for me.
And then something occurred
Crystal clear, hard, and real,
A particle crumbled off my mind
And fell into the eyes of my existence

This is when I laughed
I could have cried really
But now I laughed
I knew now where
I could find me

It would be there
Yes right there
Snapped still
At the sure sign stop
Of my cycle to the East
And I would be sitting there
On that far out Western fringe
With my me cosily tucked away
For then my life's gadflies
Of shady tomorrows & faded yesterdays
Would all be a frozen lonely track
Simply leading me
To my newly found me
At death's inevitable terminal

The African Train

Antonio Agostinho Neto

A train
climbs the rigorous African hill
halting
slow and grotesque

Screams, your screams

trying hard not to lose
but never winning

Too many lives
water the earth
where the rails lie heavily
and are crushed under the weight of the machine
and in the noise of third coach

Screams, your screams

trying hard not to lose
but never winning

slow and grotesque
African train

TRANSLATED BY BUBAKAR ADJALI

Saturdays at the Muceques

The muceques are poor neighborhoods
for poor people

come Saturday
and instantly they mingle with real life
become despair
hope and ancient myths

anguish encountered
in the meaning of things
and beings

in the full moon
relit time and again by the street lights
of the public service system
how well poverty and the full moon
blend

anguish
heard in the clamor
and in the smell of alcohol
vanished in the air
mixed with the cries of pain and joy
in the strange orchestration

anguish
of the man in uniform
endebting other men
dominating and gathering insults
and after sucking blood
throws his chest out in satisfaction
for mistreating a man

others avoid passing
where a club has struck a man
detour away
graze the walls
their backs bent over
their bare feet cut
by pieces of glass of bottles
broken by innocent children
and every woman heaves a sigh of relief
when her man comes home

anguish
of the soldiers playing
as they lie in ambush in the shadow of the cashew tree
waiting for the unknowing passer-by

> now and then
> the cries of pain
> pierce the ears
> wound the timid hearts
> drive the steps
> in an anguishing race
> after the laughter of the crowd
> uncontrollable
> only the mysterious silence of hatred's tears
> and the lacerated flesh
> by the belt buckles

anguish
which we, passers-by,
can purchase cheaply

anguish of the man
hiding in the dark corners
of the mistreated child
> his wealth silences the father
> and the child

only at night
frees his cry against fate

anguish felt
at the bar counters

TRANSLATED BY BUBAKAR ADJALI

The Green of the Palm Groves of My Youth

The canoes meandered lightly
down the dirty waters
pushing along scorias and rot
flowers, tree trunks, viscera,
propelled by fear
and labor of arms

higher! higher!
in the eyes adventure plays
in the clenched hands, terror
in the feet insecurity dances on

The Cuanza carrying along
menace and despotism
penetrates into the earth
partly flooded by torrential rains
and the crocodiles
the conquered elements
have gone to feast in the abandoned mews

Me, I run away to the green
to the black green of the palm groves
of my youth

All the gods of the centuries old mystique
and their sacrifices
bloody and peaceful
the metaphysical life of the sacred forests
the divine inspiration of the incantations
and the witch doctor
have remained, remained caught in the waters
of insecurity who is leading my feet to dance

Also remained
the religious orgies of the dead
the beautiful omens of the evil spells
hysteria
of the twilight ceremonies for life
and for death
the acrid smell of blood
the earth's fertility
the object become god
colors and dust
drops and pieces of bone
tears and songs
inviolated secrets of mysterious sects
of the human and the inhuman
poetry
and the spiritual remains of blood

Me
I innocently caressed insecurity's finger

Prayer:
Tata ietu uala ku diulu
fukamentu!
lengenu!
O ituxi! o ituxi!
O paradox of sinners!

New language!
with no stories to tell in the shade

of the "mafumeira"
or in the soft glow of a smoldering fire
not even a monkey or a lion
a rabbit or a turtle

Escape!
let the reptiles feast in the mews
abandoned
with all those who have cultivated years
and memories
of the graceful legs and bodies
of the hips and the voices
in the diminishing darkness of the night
by the fire's glow
the vibrations the rhythm
the groves of the coconut trees
the fragrance of wet and grassy earth
the voices of men
the spirit
the beauty of the genuine and the real
played upon the "marimbas" and the "quissanges"
and punctuated by the drums
sweet flavors, joys of tradition

Me, I ran away
and the spirit was caught
in the abandoned mews

defying Beethoven's symphonies
the poems my friend Mussunda doesn't understand

Me, I ran away
in the black green of the palm tree groves
of my youth
caressing insecurity's finger

the backs
the symmetrical backs bent over the earth

nursing it with the rudimentary picks
of shiny brilliance
and the songs punctuating the efforts
and the toil
and the multiple effects
the thick tears of the rootless tree trunks
and the ancient solidarity of the canoes unleashed
along the waters
and the smiles orchestrated under the screens of
the coconut trees
or the impossible attempts to embrace the "imbondeiro"
with the arms

All this was left behind
back there in Africa
in the Africa of Africa
and the cruel and destructive waters
in the abandoned mews let quench
the indecent thirst of the animals

Me, I ran away
smiling and empty
with no land no language no country
playing with adventure
how terrible the oscillation of the fragile canoes
promising
by a mystical force of conjecture
with an empty stomach
and the spirit
crushed between the putrid odor of teeth

higher!
higher!
carrying in the blood the joys of open spaces
the fragrance of bodies sacrificed for humanity
the virgin flowers
the anguish of the prison

and ignorance of fear
of the gods and of men
of the living and the dead
the fear of depths and of heights

carried in the blood
the human warmth of friendship
the feverish warmth of the violent rhythms of the night
and the brilliant green of the grass
and of the wild eyes of the "avesinhas"
the clamor of the waterfalls
and the suddenness of lightning
the earth
and man

carried in the blood
love

TRANSLATED BY BUBAKAR ADJALI

The Tide That from the West
Washes Africa to the Bone

David Rubadiri

The tide that from the west
Washes Africa to the bone
Gurgles through my ribs
And gathers the bones
That clatter into clusters,
Rough and polished,
To fling them back destitute
To the desolate river bank.

The tide that from the west
Tears through the heart sinews of Africa
Boils in my marrow,
Dissolving bone and sinew.

The tide that from the west
Washes the soul of Africa
And tears the mooring of its spirit,
Till bloodred the tide becomes
And heartsick the womb—
The tide that from the west
With blood washes Africa
Once washed a wooden cross.

On Meeting a West Indian Boat
Train at Waterloo Station

Broken, you stand and dream,
Dreams you dreamt
—And will dream—
Of new worlds to conquer
Worlds to rule
—And worlds to lose.

But your dreams
Are only dreams,
Colonnades of the mind,
Clandestine pillars
That soon lie shattered
In fertile imaginations.

Why in space build to break?
Here are no new worlds,
No new truths,
No new identity
But only
An old world
That speaks the same truths.

Here in the land of your dreams
Chimney pots
And TV masts scrape the skies
And you—
The new burrowed humanity—
Will creep each day

Like vermin
To work.

The sun spirit knows no prisons
Or casements of formality,
But you dream of dreams
As a child builds sandcastle
To break.

Thoughts After Work

Clear laughter of African children
Rings loud in the evening;
Here around this musty village
Evening falls like a mantle,
Gracing all in a shroud of peace.
Heavily from my office
I walk
To my village,
My brick government compound,
To my new exile.
In this other compound
I would no longer intrude.
I perch over a chasm,
Ride a storm I cannot hold,
And so must pass on quietly—
The laughter of children rings loud
Bringing back to me
Simple joys I once knew.

Ogunoba's Talking Drum

Scratching fussily
Like a chicken looking for seed
Into the heart of Ibadan
Where Ogunoba lived,
Like traitors
Daggers-drawn
Yet afraid (of what?),
We knew not
We were looking for a talking drum.

We sat
Dutifully broke a kola nut,
Two worlds,
East and West—
Both African.

A drum,
We wanted a drum—
Just a drum
Like tourists crying
For a cowrie shell.

Was this a cry,
A longing
Or a conquering wish?
Groping in the dark
Wishing to say
Something
Infinitely impulsive,
Childishly silly?

It came
With a message
That scuffled time beyond time.
There was bargaining,
Mere talk beyond time
A form without meaning,
A bedcover for truth;
Ogunoba broke into tears
Blessing the drum
That would fly
To the East—
A prayer
Spanning the ages of definitive African politics.

Kampala Beggar

Dark twisted form
Of shreds and cunning
Crawling with an inward twinkle
At the agonies of Africa.

Praying and pricing
Passers-by
As in black and white
Jingle pennies past;

A hawk's eye
Penetrates to the core
On a hot afternoon
To pick the victims
That with a mission
Dare not look at
This conflict.

A dollar drops,
An Indian sulk
Passively avoids—
I am stabbed to the core,
Pride rationally injured.

In the orbits of our experience
Our beggarness meets
With the clang of symbols,
Beggarly we understand
As naturally we both know
The Kampala beggar
Is wise.

Brush-fire

Tchikaya U Tam'si

The fire the river that's to say
the sea to drink following the sand
the feet the hands
within the heart to love
this river that lives in me repeoples me
only to you I said around the fire

my race
it flows here and there a river
the flames are the looks
of those who brood upon it
I said to you
my race
remembers
the taste of bronze drunk hot.

Three Poems from *Epitomé*

A bouquet of faded flowers in my letterbox . . .

I was naked for the first kiss of my mother
I was naked before Sammy and before men
I would be cold already
without this taste of black salt
in your black blood

I have the claws of a woman in my flesh
I bleed for her delight in love

But hide from me the image of her god
that fakir whose grin desalts my soul
and let the ferns
hold in the earth
the freshness of a patch of violent water.

These flowers in my letterbox, I cross my fingers to caress them
and the conscience of the world is silent with me over the drama
of Leopoldville—I spit into the Seine like all good poets.

What do I want with a thousand stars in broad daylight
the rapt surrealist
in one of them at midnight
has blessed my crazy reason

My reason is the memory of a levitation
it knits a blue stocking for the violated night
it kindles hell in the black flames it ends
the purification of my sinful swan
which once fixed a halo of pollen

on the head of a lustful black crab
my reason makes me difficult and faithless
in the abstract of my passion.

My prick is not even a root of the tree,
to speak as that tree rustles
would give a rustic perfume
to the game of my flight
and put less blood on the hands of my quest.

The disasters unfold in silence
as one loved them in childhood memory
and a grey rain serves all our dreams
forcing me to become a forger
and holy assassin
despite the equinox
despite myself

despite the sorcery of the smiles
of my obedient black brothers

And then
what would you have me say of this silence
squatting beside my own conscience?

They give you what they have eaten and what they have not
known how to keep. The shadow, like them, had a certain
reticence.
I am full of spite with the sun.

You must be from my country
I see it by the tick
of your soul around the eyelashes
and besides you dance when you are sad
you must be from my country

Keep moving time is waiting to seduce us
learn from this that the oil in your lamp
is really my blood brimming up
and that, if it overflows, you mustn't light your lamp
we must have a dark corner somewhere
for our ancient orisons

All of us from the same umbilical cord
But who knows where we fetch
our awkward heads
Often the silences
reeking of iodine ravage us
with lecherous resolves
for my beardless conscience
ravage us alone.

The Scorner

I drink to your glory my god
You who have made me so sad
You have given me a people who are not distillers of gin

What wine shall I drink to your jubilate
In this country which has no vines
In this desert all the bushes are of cactus
Shall I take their crop of flowers
For flames of the burning bush of your desire
Tell me in what Egypt my people's feet lie chained

Christ I laugh at your sadness
O my sweet Christ
Thorn for thorn
We have a common crown of thorns
I will be converted because you tempt me
Joseph comes to me
I suck already the breast of the Virgin your mother
I count more than your one Judas on my fingers
My eyes lie to my soul
Where the world is a lamb your pascal lamb—Christ
I will waltz to the tune of your slow sadness.

FROM THE WEST

Here too the white footprints
& "the brutality of appetites"
Skeletons rattle under them

Cornfields in Accra

Ama Ata Aidoo

They told us
Our mothers told us
They told us.

They told us
Our fathers told us
They told us.

They told us
Red clay
Will shine,
Shine silica,
Shine gold
Red clay will shine

It will shine
Where you polish
How-when-where
You polish.

They told us
Our mothers told us
They told us.

And so
We planted our corn:
Not whole seeds from
Last year's harvest
No,
For we are men without barns
Women without fallows.

Some said,
Referring to the corn-seeds,

"They come from Russia"
Others that the bags were marked
"Nigeria."
But we have refused to listen
Or hearing,
Have not cared.

For
When Yaa looked over her courtyard and saw Akosua's
daughter passing by with her trayful of red clay that
shone and gleamed, did she not beg a mould?
And did she wait until she knew which pit had yielded the clay?

They told us
Our mothers told us
They told us.

And we thought
As we fixed the pipe—
They said it will carry
50,000 cc. of water every day—
We thought
As we fixed the pipe,
"The first day it rains
We shall plant
The corn."

Plot One
Was Nikoi's
It was at the backyard
Where once stood the fitter's
shop:
There,
Among skeleton cars,
Greased and petrolled earth,
Bits of tyres, really
All types of scrap-metal.

The rest,
Hmm, brother,
Was less, not more
Dignified.
Mine was by a mango tree,
A hillock of rubbish dump
A deserted vacant-lot,
With unmentionable contents of diverse chamber-pots.

Yet
Even now
When that moon has not fully died
Which rose on our planting,
Let us sing of
Dark green wavy corn.

My brother,
My sister,
Take the refrain,
Swell the chorus,

They told us
Our mothers told us
They told us.

Finally,
When we have harvested, gleaned and
Threshed our corn,
Or roasted it aromatic,
That is,
After office hours
On Saturdays and throughout the whole of Sunday,
We shall sit firmly on our bottoms
And plant our feet on the earth,

Then
We shall ask to see
Him

Who says
We
Shall not survive among these turbines.

Who
Says
We shall not survive among the turbines?

Desire

Kofi Awoonor

The stars are above, stilted like merry bells;
The scented dew falls on the rotten leaves of yesterday's storm:
And I look into the herb pot to read the message from beyond.
There is no voice, no ghosts whisper.
Only the voices of the fishermen dragging the mackerel net
Beating time on the calabash drums.
In songs that ring of the sea before them
Where, where could it be?
Where gone?
The merry village clown calls me by name,
And gives me a coloured cowrie
"In the coloured cowrie you hear the sea
And are throbbing vibrations of your own soul."
But where, where could it be?
The day stands still as the years roll past
And fix me in the single quest,
For what
Is it you are looking for
In these scattered ashes from forgotten hearths?
And in the fireplace where mother's cooking pot hangs
Revealing past travails and future glories
Glories? Who says they are glories?
Behind me I smell their talcumed bodies
Washed in palm olives.
The cloths smell with camphor removed
Yesterday from the old lady's box.
They say at the journey's end there is a resting place
Covered with dead cows and hungry vultures
Who do not give you a chance
Yes a chance to measure your own limitations

Besides your future glories
The pall bearers reek with drink and vomit
And the dead man wakes up looks at them
And dies again
The glow-worm shows your way to the place of skulls
And there you find yourself reclining in an arm-chair
Supervising the ceremony of the lost
Yes the ceremony of the bewildered
The wanderers that lost their way homewards
And chose the scented putrefaction of death.

Delight of Tears

Nothing can surpass the deluge
The delight of tears and the prelude
To the seedy laughter of the asthmatic.
The boatman's scanty meals
Will survive all feasts.
He will return to find the feasters gone
And the ferryman's daughter
Married to the chief's bailiff
And the landlord's yearly rent of corn unpaid.
The deluge, the delight of tears will come again.
Marching like victorious armies
Into the untenanted land
Knocking on the door that will yield
Only to the kicks from worn out feet.
We sat at the cross-roads.
The morning star did not rise then.
And we wished to return
Shed tears of joy

Wept for the return
Of friends from distant lands
Drunk with alien wines.

The Cathedral

On this dirty patch
a tree once stood
shedding incense on the infant corn:
its boughs stretched across a heaven
brightened by the last fires of a tribe.
They sent surveyors and builders
who cut that tree
planting in its place
a huge senseless cathedral of doom.

Lament of the Silent Sister

> For Chris Okigbo, the well-known poet,
> killed in 1967 in the Nigerian Civil war.

That night he came home, he came unto me
at the cold hour of the night
Smelling of corn wine in the dawn dew.
He stretched his hand and covered my forehead.
There was a moonbeam sparking rays in particles.
The drummer boys had got themselves a goat.
The din was high in the wail of the harvest moon.

The flood was up gurgling through the fields
Birth waters swimming in floods of new blood.
He whispered my name in a far echo
Sky-wailing into a million sounds
across my shores. His voice still bore
the sadness of the wanderer
To wail and die in a soft lonely echo
That echo I heard long ago
In the fall of night over my river,
In the distant rustle of reeds
At growth in the strength of my river
Once upon an evening I heard it
Strung clear as the gong of the drummer boys
Bright burnished like the glint edge of
the paschal knife, ready anxious to cut
My cords and enter into my fields.

I was still a dream then
Carried by the flimsy whiffs
Of sweet scents borne aloft on the vision
Of my coming flood
That will bear me slowly and gently
Into his world of smiles and smells.
He was not very gentle with me
But I did not complain. The thrust
was hard and angry, severing the tiny cord
Shattering the closed gates of raffia
gathering at its eye the reeds to feed my fishes.
My flood had not risen.
The canoe carried on the strength
Of his man rowed steep down my river
into a tumultuous eternity
Of green hills and mountains
That reeled and rolled to the river shore
To clasp and bear me away.

Then the floodgates opened
for sluices to cleanse to purify
My evening of awakening
In the turbulence of his triumph
Into the bright evening of my rebirth.
The birth was tedious
The pangs were bitter
Into the bright evening I rushed
Crying I have found him I have found him.
He stood there rustling in the wind
The desire to go was written large upon his forehead.
I was not ready for his coming
I was not ready for his loneliness,
for his sad solitude against the rustling wind.
I was not ready for his entrance
Into my fields and shores of my river.
The entrance of raffia was closed
closed against his lonely solitude.

He stood beneath my entrance
In his approach I knew the steps he took
Like departing Lazarus
Marching towards his grave.
I was not ready.
The flood was gurgling at the estuary
swimming within me birthwaters
warmed by his coming. He was silent
mute against the rushing of the wind
to cry and die for his homeland.

My flood had not risen then.
Across my vastness he marched into the wind
his arms folded upon his chest,
his eyes searching for the gates
that will open his amulets
to snatch and wear his talisman of hope.

He marched into the wind
howling through door posts
to catch the boat man at the dawn point
to ferry him across my river.
But I was not ready.

My hands stretched to cover his
in the darkness, to cover his eyes
in the agony of his solitude
to call his names I knew
to put the dressing from my womb
Upon his cudgel scars,
to hold his hand in the clasp of night fall.
He was mute; the wind had stopped rustling
He was erect like the totem pole of his household
He burned and blazed for an ending.
Then I was ready. As he pierced my agony
with his cry, my river burst into flood.
My shores reeled and rolled
to the world's end, where they say
at the world's end the graves are green.

Song

J. P. Clark

I CAN LOOK the sun in the face
But the friends that I have lost
I dare not look at any. Yet I have held
Them all in my arms, shared with them
The same bath and bed, often
Devouring the same dish, drunk as soon
On tea as on wine, at that time
When but to think of an ill, made
By God or man, was to find
The cure prophet and physician
Did not have. Yet to look
At them now I dare not,
Though I can look the sun in the face.

Skulls and Cups

"LOOK, JP,
How do you tell a skull
From another?" asked Obi.
"That this, could you find where he fell,
Was Chris, that Sam, and
This there in the sand
Of course Emman. Oh yes,
How does one tell a cup on the floor
From another, when the spirit is emptied?"
And the goblets are legion,
Broken upon the fields after Nsukka.

Seasons of Omens

WHEN CALABASHES HELD petrol and men
  turned faggots in the streets
Then came the five hunters
When mansions and limousines made
  bonfires in sunset cities
Then came the five hunters
When clans were discovered that were not in the book
  and cattle counted for heads of men
Then came the five hunters
When hoodlums took possession of police barracks
  in defiance of bullets
Then came the five hunters
When ministers legislated from bed and
  made high office the prize for failure
Then came the five hunters
When wads of notes were kept in infant skulls
  with full blessing of prelates
Then came the five hunters
When women grew heavy with ballot papers delivering
  the house entire to adulterers
Then came the five hunters
When a grand vizier in season of arson turned
  upon bandits in a far off place
Then came the five hunters
When men lost their teeth before they cut them
  to eat corn
Then came the five hunters

When a cabinet grew so broad the top gave way
   and trapped everyone therein
Then came the five hunters

At club closure,
Antelopes slept, for lions snored;
Then struck the five hunters,
But not together, not together.
One set out on his own into the night,
Four down their different spoors by the sea;
By light of stars at dawn
Each read in the plan a variant

And so one morning
The people woke up to a great smoke.
There was fire all right,
But who lighted it, where
The lighter of the fire?

Fallen in the grass was the lion,
Fallen in the forest was the jackal,
Missing by the sea was the shepherd-sheep,
His castrate ram in tow,
And all around was the blood of hounds.

Dirge

SHOW ME A house where nobody has died
Death is what you cannot undo
Yet a son is killed and a daughter is given
Out of one seed springs the tree
A tree in a mad act is cut down
Must the forest fall with it?

Earth will turn a desert
A place of stone and bones
Tears are founts from the heart
Tears do not water a land
Fear too is a child of the heart
Fear piles up stones, piles up bones
Fear builds a place of ruin
O let us light the funeral pile
But let us not become its faggot
O let us charcoal the mad cutters of teak
But let us not cut down the clan!

Death of a Weaverbird

SHOT,
At Akwebe,
A place not even on the map
Made available by Shell-BP,
A weaverbird,
Whose inverted house
Had a straw from every soil.
Clear was his voice as the siren's
Chirp with no fixed hour
Of ditty or discourse . . .
When plucked,
In his throat was a note
With a bullet for another:
I am in contact with the black-kite,
At the head of a flock I have led
To this pass.
How can I return to sing another song?
To help start a counter surge?

Party Song

HERE WE MILL drinking by midnight
Here we mill bobbing by fairylight
Here we mill glowing by dimlight

A floor away
Other drums are beating
Other lamps are burning
In a titanic ball

And through open gates by night and day
Brigades and villages are going out
Like lights over Lagos

The Casualties

To Chinua Achebe

THE CASUALTIES ARE not only those who are dead;
They are well out of it.
The casualties are not only those who are wounded,
Though they await burial by instalment.
The casualties are not only those who have lost
Persons or property, hard as it is
To grope for a touch that some
May not know is not there.
The casualties are not only those led away by night;

The cell is a cruel place, sometimes a haven,
Nowhere as absolute as the grave.
The casualties are not only those who started
A fire and now cannot put it out. Thousands
Are burning that had no say in the matter.
The casualties are not only those who escaping
The shattered shell become prisoners in
A fortress of falling walls.

The casualties are many, and a good number well
Outside the scenes of ravage and wreck;
They are the emissaries of rift,
So smug in smoke-rooms they haunt abroad,
They do not see the funeral piles
At home eating up the forests.
They are the wandering minstrels who, beating on
The drums of the human heart, draw the world
Into a dance with rites it does not know

The drums overwhelm the guns . . .
Caught in the clash of counter claims and charges
When not in the niche others have left,
We fall,
All casualties of the war,
Because we cannot hear each other speak,
Because eyes have ceased to see the face from the crowd,
Because whether we know or
Do not know the extent of wrong on all sides,
We are characters now other than before
The war began, the stay-at-home unsettled
By taxes and rumours, the looters for office
And wares, fearful everyday the owners may return,
We are all casualties,
All sagging as are
The cases celebrated for kwashiorkor,
The unforeseen camp-follower of not just our war.

To My Academic Friends
Who Sit Tight on Their
Doctoral Theses and Have
No Chair for Poet or Inventor

YOU WHO WILL drive forward
But look to the rear mirror
Look at the crashes and
Casualties holding up traffic
To the market. He drives
Well who arrives
Again and again with fresh goods.

For My Mother

David Diop

When all about me memories arise
Memories of anxious hangings on the edge of cliffs
Of icy seas where harvests drown
When drifting days come back to me
Ragged days with a narcotic taste
When the word becomes aristocrat
To overcome the emptiness
Behind closed blinds
Then mother I think of you
Of your beautiful eyelids burnt by the years
Of your smile on my hospital nights
Your smile that told of old and vanquished miseries
O mother mine mother of us all
Of the Negro they blinded who once again sees flowers
Listen listen to your voice
This cry shot through with violence
This song that springs only from love.

The Vultures

There once was a time
When with civilization's ugly blows
With the spread of holy water upon domesticated brows
The vultures built in the shadows of their claws
The bleeding monuments to their tutelary era

There once was a time
When laughter was drowned in the metallic hell of roads
And the monotonous rhythm of *Pater-Nosters*
Covered the screams that rose from the plantations

O the acid memory of torn embraces
Promises mutilated by machine-gun fire

Strange men
You were not men
You knew all the books
You knew not love

While our hands made pregnant the belly of the earth
The roots of our hands went as deep as revolt

Despite your proud songs in the midst of your carnals
Desolated villages, Africa so shackled
Hope lived within us like a citadel
And from Swaziland's mines to Europe's sweat-filled factories
Springtime will be born beneath our light steps.

Times

There are times for dreaming
In the peacefulness of nights with hollow silences
And times for doubt
When the heavy web of words is torn with sighs
There are times for suffering
Along the roads of war at the look in mothers' eyes
There are times for love
In lighted huts where one flesh sings
There is what colours times to come

As sunshine greens the plants
In the delirium of these hours
In the impatience of these hours
Is the ever fertile seed
Of times when equilibrium is born

With You

With you I have refound my name
My name long hidden neath the salt of distances
I have rediscovered eyes no longer fever-dimmed
And your laughter like a flame piercing the darkness
Once more has brought me Africa despite the snows of yesterday
Ten years my love
Mornings of illusion and the remnants of ideas
And sleep inhabited by alcohol
Ten years and the breathing of the world has poured its pain on
  me
This suffering that weights the present with tomorrow's taste
And makes of love a boundless river
With you I have refound the memory of my blood
And necklaces of laughter round my days
Days that sparkle with joys renewed.

The Renegade

My brother with the teeth that gleam at hypocritical compliments
My brother with the gold-rimmed eyes that reflect the Master's
  blue ones

My poor brother in the silk-faced dinner jacket
Squealing murmuring and strutting in condescending drawing
  rooms
We pity you
The sunshine of your homeland is but a shadow now
On your brow serenely civilized
And your grandmother's hut
Would make a face turned white by years of humiliation and *mea
  culpa*
Blush
But when
Full of sonorous and empty words
Like the great drum that stands upon your shoulders
You tread the red and bitter earth of Africa
These anguished words will mark the beat of your uneasy steps
I feel alone, so lonely here!

Africa

TO MY MOTHER

Africa my Africa
Africa of proud warriors in ancestral savannas
Africa my grandmother sings of on a distant riverbank
I have never known you
But my face is filled with your blood
Your beautiful black blood spread across the fields
The blood of your sweat
The sweat of your toils
The toils of your slavery
The slavery of your children
Africa tell me Africa
Is it yours this back that is bending

Bowed low by humility's weight
This trembling red zebra-striped back
Saying yes to the whip on the sweltering roads
Then gravely a voice answered me
Impetuous son this young and robust tree
This very tree
In splendid isolation
Amid the white and wilted flowers
Is Africa your Africa growing again
Patiently stubbornly rising again
And little by little whose fruit
Bears freedom's bitter flavour.

Rama Kam

SONG FOR A BLACK WOMAN

The wildness of your glances pleases me
Your mouth has the taste of mango
    Rama Kam
Your body is the black pimento
That makes desire sing
    Rama Kam
As you pass
The handsomest woman is made jealous
By the warm rhythm of your hips
    Rama Kam
As you dance
To the tom-tom Rama Kam
The tom-tom taut as my victorious sex
Throbs beneath the griot's leaping fingers

When you love me Rama Kam
A tornado shakes
In the fiery blackness of your flesh
And fills me with your breath
    O Rama Kam!

Negro Tramp

FOR AIMÉ CÉSAIRE

You who walked like a broken old dream
Laid low by the mistral's blades
Along what salty paths
Along what detours muddy with suffering accepted
Aboard what caravels from isle to isle planting flags of Negro
    blood torn away from Guinea
Have you worn your cast-off cloak of thorns
To the foreign graveyard where you used to read the sky
In your eyes I see you halt, stooped and in despair
And dawns when cotton and the mines began again
I see Soundiata the forgotten
And the indomitable Chaka
Hidden neath the seas with the tales of silk and fire
All this I see
Martial music and the clarion call to murder
And bellies gaping open in snowy countrysides
To pacify the fear cowering in the cities
O my old Negro harvester of unknown lands
Sweet scented lands where everyone could live
What have they made of the dawn that used to open on your brow
Of your luminous stones and golden sabres
Look at you naked in your filthy prison

A dead volcano for others to laugh at
For others to get rich on
To feed their awful hunger
Whitey they called you how picturesque
Shaking their fat, high-principled heads
Pleased with their joke, not nasty at all
But I, what did I do on your windy weeping morning
That morning drowned in seafoam
When the sacred cows decayed
What did I do seated on my clouds but tolerate
The nocturnal dyings
The immutable wounds
The petrified rags in the terror stricken camps
The sand seemed made of blood
And I saw a day like any other day
And I sang Yeba
Yeba like a raving animal
O buried plants
O lost seeds
Forgive me Negro guide
Forgive my narrow heart
The victories postponed the armour abandoned
Patience the Carnival is done
I am sharpening a hurricane to plough the future with
For you we shall remake Ghana and Timbuktu
And guitars will galop wildly
In great shuddering chords
Like the hammerblows of pestles
Pounding mortars
Bursting forth
From hut to hut
Into the portentive blue.

Veterans Day

Ifeanyi Menkiti

And because somebody
fired a gun
at somebody else
at Sarajevo;
but more because
of a man named Darwin,
who said his daddy
was an ape,
and proved it in a book;

therefore did the nations
fight amongst themselves
to decide who was fittest to survive
and killed a few million people
among whom were Africans
conscripted to serve;

bloodied, that is, to prove a point
concerning civilization's
monkey-mongering ways.

Adaiba

The clear stream in the clear day
shall flow with her return;
and may the glow escort her,
as I rise to meet her;
the deep one gird with god-light.

For Malcolm

Some slaves survived
  giving birth to "Negroes";
some "Negroes" will survive
  giving birth to BLACK MEN.

Malcolm be content
rest
  assured there in your grave.

Blonde Bondage

"If I've only one life to live
  let me live it as a blonde . . ."

And for four hundred years,
bleaching to become blondes,
out-whiters of Arya,
the warped daughters of bondage

Emmy Lou, out of tune with her own;
her hair botched from black to white,
her skin a chemical transformation;
that she might wear the pale glow
and walk at eve with the prima donnas:

          the sick act,
          the troubled rash
                    of exile.

Grace Before Meal
(for my missionary friends)

God of meatloaves, winecups, fleshpots, and of pleasure
                    glory be Thy name;
and blessed be they who suffer duodenal ulcers
                    for the Gospel's sake.

The Drunken Priest

Flower of the Church
triumphant in Africa
thriving on alcohol

And All Shall Be Well

Citizens of law and order,
he who must break the law
must first invite the cop to tea
and the Lord Chief Justice to dinner.

The Pagans Sat Still

I

In the beginning was the Word,
and the Word was to spread,
alike to the shod and unshod.
In the beginning was the Word.

In the beginning was the Word,
the quite correct concept of man,
the divine,
the very white.
In the beginning was the Word.

"Vanity of vanities" said the preacher
and there is no end to the making of books—

The pagan ages brought damnation"
    so ancient mounds of ancestors are vilified;
"The christian ages bring redemption"
    and psychotic babble supplants Ezani's arcana.

             In the beginning was the Word.

And they planted God in Africa,
and they fertilized him with Europa,
hoping for a bumper harvest,
returns of the sacred interest.

II

The pagans sat still while they instilled,
sat still as heaven-inspired omniscience
    rolled into their ears—
all they shall unlearn later.

Came swarms with creeds untested,
soldiers of New Conversions,
sectarians of the Lord,
preaching brotherhood, then reneging,
    shocked the children of the sun;
preaching gentleness, then forgetting,
    ripped off, cast *ikenga* to the flames:

            iconoclasts of baffled creeds,
            grubs feeding on mysteries arcane.

Woe unto you hypocrites,
lechers in virgin skirts,
rapists in sheep's clothing.

There was no tropic stance,
no value, no manhood,
they did not desecrate;
in arrogance imposing alien testaments,
an unweaned phrase of life taught absolute code,
an unformed set of dreams taught inspired truth:

            the god they brought a god with gout
            an aging deity with diapered pants—

Lies told in the old soil,
lies told in the old soil,
ad maiorem gloriam Dei, in any case;
in any case ad maiorem gloriam Dei.

Wisdom of the ages!
rancid loaves from Middle Ages,
in sickened juvenescence brought tropic homes;
in alien suppositories choking the sensitivity
    of an age:

            corruptibility taking on corruption
            detumescence of worms from reverend bowels.

Presumption as never known in the old soil,
bloated arrogance peddling humility,

on Sundays preaching beatitudes,
on weekdays living sin;
by force of miracles never witnessed gaining ground;
for love of God's love preaching hell—
   Dialectics cursed in the womb.

No,
crabgrass is not for us,
wheatrot is not for us.

Flow then spirit streams,
in gentler ministration flow;

in gentler ministration flow
that *ikenga* in its return
might purge the infected hearth;
that children at twilight
might sleep on their mothers' laps,
not frightened by heavenly scowls at eve,
nor shaken by gusts of vain, infertile creeds.

Turn then alienated wand;
in primal dispensation turn.

Age of the Gods Who Never Came

Age of the gods who never came,
the rose calling, hinting, never blooming;
in season, out of season,
trailing the secret hours:
Son of man, son of man . . .

Singer, in the dark fields,
what means this burning of darkness?

and what this motion of closed years?
this projection through time in still dance?
what mean?

Son of Man,
the kingdom of God is within you;
the kingdom of God is also moving
onward and upward, in stillness,
                    into stillness.

And water also will burn;
nor will I be not willing
            to tell of this
when my song of flame is ended—

Who moved among the astral marshes,
tongue-tied, still chanting in the night.

Spirit of the Wind

Gabriel Okara

The storks are coming now—
white specks in the silent sky.
They had gone north seeking
fairer climes to build their homes
when here was raining.

They are back with me now—
spirits of the wind,
beyond the gods' confining
hands, they go north and west and east,
instinct guiding.

But willed by the gods
I'm sitting on this rock
watching them come and go
from sunrise to sundown, with the spirit
urging within.

And urging, a red pool stirs,
and each ripple is
the instinct's vital call,
desire in a million cells
confined.

O God of the gods and me,
shall I not heed
this prayer-bell call, the noon
angelus, because my stork is caged
in singed hair and dark skin?

Once Upon a Time

Once upon a time, son,
they used to laugh with their hearts
and laugh with their eyes;
but now they only laugh with their teeth,
while their ice-block-cold eyes
search behind my shadow.

There was a time indeed
they used to shake hands with their hearts;
but that's gone, son.
Now they shake hands without hearts
while their left hands search
my empty pockets.

"Feel at home," "Come again,"
they say, and when I come
again and feel
at home, once, twice,
there will be no thrice—
for then I find doors shut on me.

So I have learned many things, son.
I have learned to wear many faces
like dresses—homeface,
officeface, streetface, hostface, cocktailface,
with all their conforming smiles
like a fixed portrait smile.

And I have learned too
to laugh with only my teeth

and shake hands without my heart.
I have also learned to say "Goodbye,"
when I mean "Goodriddance";
to say "Glad to meet you,"
without being glad; and to say "It's been
nice talking to you," after being bored.

But believe me, son.
I want to be what I used to be
when I was like you. I want
to unlearn all these muting things.
Most of all, I want to relearn
how to laugh, for my laugh in the mirror
shows only my teeth like a snake's bare fangs!

So show me, son,
how to laugh; show me how
I used to laugh and smile
once upon a time when I was like you.

The Mystic Drum

The mystic drum beat in my inside
and fishes danced in the rivers
and men and women danced on land
to the rhythm of my drum—

But standing behind a tree
with leaves around her waist
she only smiled with a shake of her head.

Still my drum continued to beat,
rippling the air with quickened

tempo compelling the quick
and the dead to dance and sing
with their shadows—

But standing behind a tree
with leaves around her waist
she only smiled with a shake of her head.

Then the drum beat with the rhythm
of the things of the ground
and invoked the eye of the sky
the sun and the moon and the river gods—
and the trees began to dance,
the fishes turned men
and men turned fishes
and things stopped to grow—

But standing behind a tree
with leaves around her waist
she only smiled with a shake of her head.

And then the mystic drum
in my inside stopped to beat—
and men became men,
fishes became fishes
and trees, the sun and the moon
found their places, and the dead
went to the ground and things began to grow.

And behind the tree she stood
with roots sprouting from her
feet and leaves growing on her head
and smoke issuing from her nose
and her lips parted in her smile
turned cavity belching darkness.

Then, then I packed my mystic drum
and turned away; never more to beat so loud.

Adhiambo

I hear many voices
like it's said a madman hears;
I hear trees talking
like it's said a medicine man hears.

Maybe I'm a madman,
I'm a medicine man.

Maybe I'm mad,
for the voices are luring me,
urging me from the midnight
moon and the silence of my desk
to walk on wave crests across a sea.

Maybe I'm a medicine man
hearing talking saps,
seeing behind trees;
but who's lost his powers
of invocation.

But the voices and the trees
are now name-spelling and one figure
silence-etched across
the moonface is walking, stepping
over continents and seas.

And I raised my hand—
my trembling hand, gripping
my heart as handkerchief
and waved and waved—and waved—
but she turned her eyes away.

To Paveba

When young fingers stir
the fire smouldering in my inside
the dead weight of dead years roll
crashing to the ground
and the fire begins to flame anew.

The fire begins to flame anew
devouring the debris of years—
the dry harmattan-sucked trees,
the dry tearless faces
smiling weightless smiles like breath
that do not touch the ground.

The fire begins to flame anew
and I laugh and shout to the eye
of the sky on the back of a fish
and I stand on the wayside
smiling the smile of budding trees
at men and women whose insides
are filled with ashes, who
tell me, "We once had our flaming fire."

Then I remember my vow.
I remember my vow not to let
my fire flame any more. And the dead
years rise creaking from the ground
and file slowly into my inside
and shyly push aside the young fingers
and smother the devouring flame.

And as before the fire smoulders in water,
continually smouldering beneath
the ashes with things I dare not tell
erupting from the hackneyed lore
of the beginning. For they die in the telling.

So let them be. Let them smoulder.
Let them smoulder in the living fire beneath the ashes.

Thunder Can Break

Christopher Okigbo

FANFARE of drums, wooden bells: iron chapter;
And our dividing airs are gathered home.

This day belongs to a miracle of thunder;
Iron has carried the forum
With token gestures. Thunder has spoken,
Left no signatures: broken

Barbicans alone tell one tale the winds scatter.

Mountain or tower in sight, lo, your hostages—
Iron has made, alas, masterpieces—
Statuettes of legendary heroes—iron birds
Held—fruit of flight—tight;

For barricaded in iron handiwork a miracle caged.

Bring them out we say, bring them out
Faces and hands and feet,
The stories behind the myth, the plot
Which the ritual enacts.

Thunder can break—Earth, bind me fast—
Obduracy, the disease of elephants.

Elegy of the Wind

WHITE LIGHT, receive me your sojourner; O milky way,
    let me clasp you to my waist;
And may my muted tones of twilight
Break your iron gate, the burden of several centuries,
    into twin tremulous cotyledons . . .

Man of iron throat—for I will make broadcast with
    eunuch-horn of seven valves—
I will follow the wind to the clearing,
And with muffled steps seemingly out of breath break
    the silence the myth of her gate.

For I have lived the sappling sprung from the bed
    of the old vegetation;
Have shouldered my way through a mass of ancient
    nights to chlorophyll;

Or leaned upon a withered branch,
A blind beggar leaning on a porch.

I have lived the oracle dry on the cradle of a new generation . . .
The autocycle leans on a porch, the branch dissolves into
                                 embers,

The ashes resolve their moments
Of twin-drops of dew on a leaf:
And like motion into stillness is my divine rejoicing—
The man embodies the child
The child embodies the man; the man remembers
The song of the innocent,
Of the uncircumcised at the sight of the flaming razor—

The chief priest of the sanctuary has uttered
   the enchanted words;
The bleeding phallus,
Dripping fresh from the carnage cries out for
   the medicinal leaf . . .

O wind, swell my sails; and may my banner run
   the course of wider waters:

The child in me trembles before the high shelf
   on the wall,
The man in me shrinks before the narrow neck of
   a calabash;

And the chant, already all wings, follows
In its ivory circuit behind the thunder clouds,
The slick route of the feathered serpent . . .

Come Thunder

NOW THAT the triumphant march has entered the last street
                                      corners,
Remember, O dancers, the thunder among the clouds . . .

Now that laughter, broken in two, hangs tremulous between
                                    the teeth,
Remember, O dancers, the lightning beyond the earth . . .

The smell of blood already floats in the lavender-mist of the
                                   afternoon.
The death sentence lies in ambush along the corridors of
                                   power;
And a great fearful thing already tugs at the cables of the open
                                     air,

A nebula immense and immeasurable, a night of deep waters—
An iron dream unnamed and unprintable, a path of stone.

The drowsy heads of the pods in barren farmlands witness it,
The homesteads abandoned in this century's brush fire witness
it:
The myriad eyes of deserted corn-cobs in burning barns witness
it:
Magic birds with the miracle of lightning flash on their
feathers . . .

The arrows of God tremble at the gates of light,
The drums of curfew pander to a dance of death;

And the secret thing in its heaving
Threatens with iron mask
The last lighted torch of the century . . .

Hurrah for Thunder

WHATEVER happened to the elephant—
Hurrah for thunder—

The elephant, tetrarch of the jungle:
With a wave of the hand
He could pull four trees to the ground;
His four mortar legs pounded the earth:
Wherever they treaded,
The grass was forbidden to be there.

Alas! the elephant has fallen—
Hurrah for thunder—

But already the hunters are talking about pumpkins:
If they share the meat let them remember thunder.

The eye that looks down will surely see the nose;
The finger that fits should be used to pick the nose.

Today—for tomorrow, today becomes yesterday:
How many million promises can ever fill a basket.

If I don't learn to shut my mouth I'll soon go to hell,
I, Okigbo, town-crier, together with my iron bell.

Elegy for Slit-drum

With rattles accompaniment

CONDOLENCES . . . from our swollen lips laden with
                                    condolences:

The mythmaker accompanies us
The rattles are here with us

condolences from our split-tongue of the slit-drum condolences

one tongue full of fire
one tongue full of stone—

condolences from the twin-lips of our drum parted in
                                    condolences:

the panther has delivered a hare
the hare is beginning to leap
the panther has delivered a hare
the panther is about to pounce—

condolences already in flight under the burden of this century:

parliament has gone on leave
the members are now on bail

parliament is now on sale
the voters are lying in wait—

condolences to caress the swollen eyelids of bleeding mourners.

the cabinet has gone to hell
the timbers are now on fire
the cabinet that sold itself
ministers are now in gaol—

condolences quivering before the iron throne of a new
                                                    conqueror:

the mythmaker accompanies us (*the Egret had come and gone*)
Okigbo accompanies us the oracle enkindles us
the Hornbill is there again (*the Hornbill has had a bath*)
Okigbo accompanies us the rattles enlighten us—

condolences with the miracle of sunlight on our feathers:

The General is up . . . the General is up . . . commandments . . .
the General is up the General is up the General is up—

condolences from our twin-beaks and feathers of condolences:

the General is near the throne
an iron mask covers his face
the General has carried the day
the mortars are far away—

condolences to appease the fever of a wake among tumbled
                                                    tombs

the elephant has fallen
the mortars have won the day
the elephant has fallen
does he deserve his fate
the elephant has fallen
can we remember the date—

Jungle tanks blast Britain's last stand—

the elephant ravages the jungle
the jungle is peopled with snakes
the snake says to the squirrel
I will swallow you
the mongoose says to the snake
I will mangle you
the elephant says to the mongoose
I will strangle you

thunder fells the trees cut a path
thunder smashes them all—condolences . . .

THUNDER that has struck the elephant
the same thunder should wear a plume—condolences

a roadmaker makes a road
the road becomes a throne
can we cane him for felling a tree—condolences . . .

THUNDER that has struck the elephant
the same thunder can make a bruise—condolences:

we should forget the names
we should bury the date
the dead should bury the dead—condolences

from our bruised lips of the drum empty of condolences:

trunk of the iron tree we cry *condolences* when we break,
shells of the open sea we cry *condolences* when we shake . . .

Elegy for Alto

With drum accompaniment

AND THE HORN may now paw the air howling goodbye . . .

For the Eagles are now in sight:
Shadows in the horizon—

THE ROBBERS are here in black sudden steps of showers, of
caterpillars—

THE EAGLES have come again,
The eagles rain down on us—

POLITICIANS are back in giant hidden steps of howitzers, of
detonators—

THE EAGLES descend on us,
Bayonets and cannons—

THE ROBBERS descend on us to strip us of our laughter, of our
thunder—

THE EAGLES have chosen their game,
Taken our concubines—

POLITICIANS are here in this iron dance of mortars, of
generators—

THE EAGLES are suddenly there,
New stars of iron dawn;

So let the horn paw the air howling goodbye . . .

O mother mother Earth, unbind me; let this be
   my last testament; let this be

The ram's hidden wish to the sword the sword's
 secret prayer to the scabbard—

THE ROBBERS are back in black hidden steps of detonators—

FOR BEYOND the blare of sirened afternoons, beyond
 the motorcades;
Beyond the voices and days, the echoing highways; beyond
          the latescence
Of our dissonant airs; through our curtained eyeballs,
 through our shuttered sleep,
Onto our forgotten selves, onto our broken images;
 beyond the barricades
Commandments and edicts, beyond the iron tables,
 beyond the elephant's
Legendary patience, beyond his inviolable bronze
 bust; beyond our crumbling towers—

BEYOND the iron path careering along the same beaten track—

THE GLIMPSE of a dream lies smouldering in a cave,
 together with the mortally wounded birds.
Earth, unbind me; let me be the prodigal; let this be
 the ram's ultimate prayer to the tether . . .

AN OLD STAR departs, leaves us here on the shore
Gazing heavenward for a new star approaching;
The new star appears, foreshadows its going
Before a going and coming that goes on forever . . .

Koko Oloro

Wole Soyinka

From a children's propitiation chant

Dolorous knot
Plead for me
Farm or hill
Plead for me
Stream and wind
Take my voice
Home or road
Plead for me
On this shoot, I
Bind your leaves
Stalk and bud
Berries three
On the threshold
Cast my voice
Knot of bitters
Plead for me.

Post Mortem

there are more functions to a freezing plant
than stocking beer; cold biers of mortuaries
submit their dues, harnessed—glory be!—

is the cold hand of death . . .
his mouth was cotton filled, his man-pike
shrunk to sub-soil grub

his head was hollowed and his brain
on scales—was this a trick to prove
fore-knowledge after death?

his flesh confesses what has stilled
his tongue; masked fingers think from him
to learn, how not to die.

let us love all things of grey; grey slabs
grey scalpel, one grey sleep and form,
grey images.

Black Singer

for Marge, New York

Cold wreath of vine, darkly
Coiled about the night; echoes deep within
Bled veins of autumn

A votive vase, her throat
Poured many souls as one; how dark
The wine became the night.

Fleshed from out disjointed, out from
The sidewalk hurt of sirens, a darkling
Pool of wine shivers

In light shrapnels, and do you ask
How *is* the wine tonight? Dark, lady
Dark in token of the deeper wounds

Full again of promises
Of the deep and silent wounds
Of cruel phases of the darksome wine

Song, O Voice, is lonely envoy
Night a runnel for the wine's indifferent flow.

Civilian and Soldier

My apparition rose from the fall of lead,
Declared, "I'm a civilian." It only served
To aggravate your fright. For how could I
Have risen, a being of this world, in that hour
Of impartial death! And I thought also: nor is
Your quarrel of this world.
                              You stood still
For both eternities, and oh I heard the lesson
Of your training sessions, cautioning—
Scorch earth behind you, do not leave
A dubious neutral to the rear. Reiteration
Of my civilian quandry, burrowing earth
From the lead festival of your more eager friends
Worked the worse on your confusion, and when
You brought the gun to bear on me, and death
Twitched me gently in the eye, your plight
And all of you came clear to me.
                              I hope some day
Intent upon my trade of living, to be checked
In stride by *your* apparition in a trench,
Signalling, I am a soldier. No hesitation then
But I shall shoot you clean and fair
With meat and bread, a gourd of wine
A bunch of breasts from either arm, and that
Lone question—do you friend, even now, know
What it is all about?

Biographies

Ama Ata Aidoo was born at Abeadzi Kyiakor in the Central Region of Ghana. She was educated at the University of Ghana where she received her B.A. She was appointed a Research Fellow of the Institute of African Studies and attended the Advanced Creative Writing Course at Stanford University in California. She has published a collection of short stories, *No Sweetness Here* (Doubleday) and two plays. She is currently a lecturer at the University of Ghana, Cape Coast.

Kofi Awoonor was born in Ghana and attended the University College of Ghana and the University College of London, where he held the Longmans Fellowship. He has published a novel, *This Earth My Brother,* two collections of poetry, *Rediscovery* and *Night of My Blood,* and a collection of plays, *Ancestral Power.* He is currently teaching at S.U.N.Y. in Stonybrook, Long Island, where he started the African Literature Program and where he is also the director of the Comparative Literature Program.

Dennis Brutus was born in Rhodesia. He has published three volumes of poetry: *Sirens, Knuckles and Boots, Letters to Martha,* and *Poems From Algiers.* He wrote *Letters to Martha* while he was in jail for trying to fight against apartheid. He is director of the World Campaign for the Release of South African Political Prisoners.

J. P. Clark was born in 1935 at Kiagbodo in Midwestern Nigeria. He has published three books of poetry: *Poems, A Reed in the Tide* and *Casualties,* several plays, among them, *Ozidi* and *Three Plays* ("Song of a Goat," "The Masquerade," and "The Raft") and his assessment of America, *America Their America.* J. P. Clark is co-editor of *Black Orpheus,* and he teaches in Lagos.

Solomon Deressa writes in Amharic, French, and English. The poems published in this anthology are from an unpublished collection of his entitled, *The Tone of Silence: A Mid-Century African Portrait*. He is head of Production Operations, Radio Ethiopia.

David Diop was born in 1927 in Bordeaux, France. He was killed in a plane crash in 1960 off Dakar. He was a regular contributor to *Presence Africaine* and had published *Coups D Pilon*—a collection of poetry.

Zweli ed Dladla was born in East London, Cape Province. He left South Africa in 1966 after spending two and a half years in prison on false charges of political crimes. Mr. Dladla holds a B.A. in Sociology from Adelphi University and is currently completing his Master's Degree in Education at the University of Massachusetts. The poems that appear in this anthology are contained in his unpublished manuscript entitled (*Of Life, Love, and Death*), *I Choose to Sing to Stones*.

Keorapetse Kgositsile was born in 1938 in Johannesburg, South Africa. He is a poet and essayist, and has been living in exile since 1961. Kgositsile was on the staff of *New Age*, a now-banned South African political weekly. He was the recipient of the second Conrad Kent Rivers Memorial Poetry Award, given by *Black World* magazine. He has published three volumes of poetry: *Spirits Unchained, For Melba*, and *My Name Is Afrika*.

Mazisi Kunene was born in 1930 in Durban, South Africa. He received his M.A. from Natal University. He is a poet, dramatist, and essayist. He won the Bantu Literary Competition in 1956. At present he is an African National Congress Representative (South Africa) in London. His selections in this anthology are from a collection entitled *Zulu Poems*.

Burns B. Machobane was born in Lesotho, South Africa in 1941. He received his B.S. from Tuskegee Institute in 1967 and his M.Ed. from the same school in 1969. Presently he is the editor of *Forum*, an educational journal. He is also a lecturer of African History at Lehigh University.

Mouloud Mammeri playwright, poet, and novelist, took part in the Algerian struggle for liberation. One of his novels, *Le Sommeil Du Juste* (The Sleep of the Just) has been translated into English. The rough translation of the prologue to his play *Le Foehn*, was done by Lewis Nkosi.

Edouard Maunick was born in 1931 in Mauritius. Maunick describes himself as a "child of a thousand races" and writes poetry in French and English. Since coming to France in 1959, he has given lectures and conferences and has been in charge of literary programs broadcast by the Office de Cooperation Radiophonique. His poetical works include, *Les Maneges de la Mer*, *Mascaret*, and *Futillez-Moi*.

Ifeanyi Menkiti was born in Onitsha, Nigeria, in 1940. He has contributed poems to several magazines in Africa and in the United States. Third World Press published his first book of poetry, *Affirmations*, in 1971. He studied at Pomona College, Columbia University, New York University, and Harvard.

Guy C. Z. Mhone is of Malawi descent and was born in Zambia. He is a graduate of Dartmouth College, where he received a B.A. in economics. Presently, Mhone is completing his Ph.D. at Syracuse University. Some of his poetry has been published in college magazines and *Greenfield Review*.

Antonio Agostinho Neto was born in 1922 at Icola e Beno in Angola. He studied medicine in Lisbon and practiced in Angola. In 1960, Neto was elected president of MPLA, the Angolan Liberation Movement. He was arrested for his activities, but in 1962 he escaped. He has been published in Portuguese and Angolan reviews and in Andrade's *Caderno* and several other anthologies.

Stella Ngatho writes of herself: "I have just finished 'A' levels. Waiting to continue my studies. Am twenty-one years of age. I hope to do speech therapy as a career."

Gabriel Okara was born in 1921 in Nigeria. He attended Government College, Umuahia. Several of his poems have appeared in

Black Orpheus and several anthologies. He has also written a novel, *The Voice* (André Deutsch, 1964).

Christopher Okigbo was born in 1932 at Ojoto in Eastern Nigeria. He was educated at Government College, Umuahia, and University College, Ibadan. He was killed during the Biafra/Nigerian War in 1967. His books of poetry include: *Heavensgate, Limits Silences,* and *Labyrinths.*

Okot p'Bitek was born in 1931 in Gulu, Northern Uganda. He attended King's College, Budo. Later he studied Law at Aberystwyth and social anthropology at Oxford, where his B.Litt. thesis on traditional songs of the Acoli and Lango was presented in 1963. He is the author of a novel, *Lak Tar Miyo Kinyero Wi Lobo* and three volumes of poetry: *Song of Lawino, Song of Ocol,* and *Song of the Prisoner.* The selection in this anthology is from *Song of Lawino.*

David Rubadiri was born in 1930 in Malawi. He attended Makerere College in Uganda and King's College, Cambridge. Mr. Rubadiri was Ambassador for Malawi to the United States until 1965, after which he joined the staff at Makerere College.

Wole Soyinka was born in 1935 at Abeokuta in Western Nigeria. He was educated in Ibadan at Government College and University College at Leeds University. He is one of the most prolific contemporary African playwrights. Among his plays are: *A Dance of the Forests, The Lion and the Jewel, The Road, The Trials of Brother Jero, The Swamp Dweller's* and *The Strong Breed.* In 1965 he published a novel entitled *The Interpreters.* His poems in this anthology are from *Idandre and Other Poems.*

Tchikaya U Tam'si was born in 1931 in Mpili in the Middle Congo. He was educated at lycées in Orléans and Paris. He has published several books of poetry among them, *Le Mauvais Sang, Feu de Brosse, A Triche Coeur,* and *Epitomé.*

INDEX OF TITLES

INDEX OF AUTHORS

INDEX OF FIRST LINES